A

YUCKY DIALOG

A

YUCKY DIALOG

Iva J. Brassfield

DEDICATION

To a Legacy of Love

Prophetess Della Daniels-Williams (02/13/1957 - 03/28/2013) was my sister from the moment we met. Our lives were so different when we came together in high school; she was a church girl, and I was the wayward girl, and we came as odd as they get. Who knew how God would intertwine our hearts as one?

Some 20 years later I became a born-again believer, and we served in ministry together. She was my greatest cheerleader, and two of the last things she said to me as she battled through the final stages of her life were, "I am so proud of you" and "finish that book." Her ability to love me unconditionally for 40 years was one of the greatest gifts I have received from God.

TABLE OF CONTENTS

ACKNOWLEDGEMENTS

My Heavenly Father: There would not be an acknowledgments page had you not first created me in the depths of your heart, and released me to planet earth with the gifts you intended for such a time as this. As I was formed in the womb of my mother, you placed specific talents and gifts within me that are unique to your plans and purpose for my life. Thank you for the gift of writing that has finally released the hidden voice within me so that I may bring words of healing to the world. Thank you for restoring my identity through your Son Jesus Christ, who transformed my life into a new creation. Thank you for loving me through my yucky past and for being the promise that evolves in me every day that I live. You are good, and your mercies endure forever.

Lucy Thelma Grace-Osbourne: My mother who has been my greatest inspiration since I hit the planet. Having earned her master's degree in her 70's and writing her first book *Quilt University* at the age of 85; she has pushed and challenged me to never be defined by my age, but to be determined by growing continuously until my last breath. Love you mommy beyond measure.

My siblings: My only big brother Nep, big sister Chay, little sisters Joy, Ashley and Tori, you know me and have allowed me to "do me" with all of my quirky ways, and I love that you are my family.

My children Candace (Akil Sr.) Jones and Giavanna Smith: You have inspired me to fight not only to live, but also to live over the fullness of time. You have stuck with me (as if you had a choice) as your mom through some of my darkest days. You have also screamed the loudest through my breakthroughs and victories. Thank you for pushing me to finish this book.

My grandchildren Legaci, Akil Jr., London Ivana (my namesake), Heiress and King: I prayed for the day you would arrive on the planet years before you ever got here. I wanted to be a praying granny and God granted me the desire of my heart. You are the reason I fought to overcome the past. I wrote this as a legacy for each of you to know you will be able to overcome anything in this life when Jesus Christ is the head of your life.

Melody Waters, my former co-pastor: Thank you so much for taking the time to read my work and give me essential feedback and encouragement to stay the course. You and *Evangelist Charles Jr.* labored with me for many years before this book was written. I love you both so much and will always be grateful for your support.

*My spiritual Dad and Mom in the Lord, **Bishop Willie and***

Evangelist Frankie Anderson (New Directions Church International, Southfield, Michigan), *thank you for pouring your unconditional love, years of wisdom and warm fellowship into me until I could stand on my own again. Love you both so much!*

Toni Rambo (my lifelong friend) and *The Leading Ladies* *morning prayer group,* thank you for the impartations and prayers throughout this writing process.

To my sista/friends and girl's night out crew, *Carol Garth-Sandefer, Gail Willis-Allen, Karen Hunt-Holmes:* In my most complex moments you never walked away from me, even when you should have been running. Instead, you have prayed with me, spoken life over me, loved on me in the moments of my writing meltdowns and committed to praying me through. I love you all so much and thank you for believing in me not just during this writing process but over the years.

To my midwives in the spirit, Evangelist Sandra Watkins, Evangelist Regina Hill, Pastor Marva Pope and Evangelist Michelle Jones: Thank you for carrying me through the difficult time of transition before the birth of my story. Love you so much.

Dr. Kimberly Butler, of Pathways to Christian Counseling in Findlay, Ohio. I am eternally grateful for the safe place presented for me to unfold my story without judgment, which enabled me to walk out the changes necessary that has brought healing to my former war-torn soul.

Dr. DeAunderia Bowens of Well and Rock Movement, LLC for her book editing work. Thank you for the professional and committed job of seeing this project through to its birth. Your keen eye and ability to edit on this level has stretched me further than I knew possible and has blessed me beyond measure. Thank you for helping me to grow in my writing; I am forever grateful.

For those not mentioned by name: Thank you for your relentless contribution of prayers, support, and encouragement.

THE DAMAGED VESSELS

As He strolled along the old-world cobblestone roads
His eyes glanced with purpose back and forth seeking the quaint
little shop that held the hidden treasures.
His steps were with great purpose and would not lead Him off
His path until He found what He came for.
Suddenly, the sun from above shown forth brightly over this
particular shop to let Him know He had arrived. He inhaled and
exhaled with calm breath, for this day He would find the
treasures His heart longed for.
He placed His hand on the doorknob and entered the little shop
and looked around.
Dust on the shelves, dirty stained-glass windows, floors
unwashed from long moments past and shelves of every color
and shape with vessels all one of a kind.
The shop owner was elderly and of feeble posture. He
approached the stranger and asked what could he help Him
with, for it was rare to get a visitor that he did not already know.
He looked and smiled at the owner of the shop and said, "Sir, I
have come for the best vessels in your shop to take
home with me today."

The owner took off his glasses and wiped them with a dirty rag from the counter and replaced them as if his vision was clearer. He then guided the stranger to the only shelf in the shop that was wiped clean with glistering new vessels on stellar display. The stranger strolled around the shelf looking for what He came for, but He was shaking His head back and forth. "No this is not what I am seeking."

The shop owner was perplexed and scratched his head trying to convince the stranger that these were the best vessels in the town on this shelf. They came from all around the world made with the best quality of materials that one could ever find. The stranger knew the real value of these new vessels, but He specifically came for the hidden treasure of damaged vessels. Looking around before He departed this little shop and found His way to the next one, He stopped and stared at the rickety sign hanging over the doorpost of a section in the back of the store.
The sign read: 'Damaged.'

The stranger's heart began to race as His pace quickened to enter that door.
Once inside He began to smile from an unspeakable joy.
He turned to the shop owner and asked, "How much for every one of these damaged and broken vessels?"

The owner said, "Sir I have many vessels on the shelf I just showed you, all with a reasonable price tag; but these old, damaged, broken-down and useless vessels are FREE! They have no value to me".

The stranger smiled and said, "Please wrap ALL of them and leave not one behind! These are the greatest treasures that you have in this shop and I have just been made rich in ways only God would know".

The shop owner began to wrap them and placed them in a crate, baffled by this sudden turn of events.

Who would ever believe that this stranger cleaned out his junk room? He quietly laughed to himself and thought, "How foolish this stranger must be?"

The stranger stood by silently, saying a prayer, thanking the Father in Heaven for guiding Him to such a vast portal of treasures on this day. He felt so blessed and honored to be the catalyst to recover and restore ALL of the chosen vessels from final and permanent destruction.

Gathering up the crate from the shop owner, He thanked him for the new-found treasures and started on His joyful journey home.

The owner of the little shop closed the door behind the unknown stranger, happy to be rid of the trash in the 'Damaged' section. Meanwhile, the stranger went back over the cobblestone roads carrying those treasures of damaged vessels to His home. His purpose on that day, as with many other days, was to retrieve and restore damaged vessels placed within His hands. He alone was the restorer of damaged goods.

Dedicated to the Hearts of True Shepherds
Iva J. Brassfield 09/30/2016

Introduction

A DREAM: June 28, 2011

I dreamed that I ventured into a forest to rescue a child in need of healing. I followed hesitantly behind Bishop Paul Morton who had gained quite a distance ahead of me. Once he made a right turn, I found myself standing at the threshold of the forest alone. As I stepped entirely through the door into the forest a stirring from above began. When I peered upward into the tall green trees, I realized the stirrings were demonic. The further I proceeded into the forest, I noticed the demons were starting to vomit and fall out of the lush, green trees.

As my confidence began to rise, so did my awareness that I was walking in authority. As I navigated a right turn I started to declare with power, "every demon must flee," and countless demons began falling out of the trees. I was startled awake by the ringing of my phone.

The call was from Pathways to Christian Counseling located in Findlay, Ohio, where I was seeking biblical counseling from Dr. Kimberly Butler. I was so excited; the phone call confirmed my sessions for "Restoring the Foundation", a prayer, restoration and deliverance ministry that was to begin on the upcoming Monday.

1

INTERPRETATION:

The dream was symbolic of the journey ahead and the results of completing the path set before me. I believe Bishop Paul Morton proceeding forward to reach the child represented Dr. Butler. The direction in the dream that I would need to follow was established, but I had to overcome fear to proceed forward. The child in need of healing was me, and the forest represented the path to my healing.

I had to go through the forest to obtain the authority to overcome. I would later learn in the 'Restoring the Foundations' ministry the four specific areas in which I needed to focus on to overcome. Those areas were *sins of the father and resulting curses, ungodly beliefs, soul/spirit hurts and demonic oppression.*

The exciting thing about all of this is that on Sunday, August 6, 2006, while visiting the bookstore at Cornerstone Church in Maumee, Ohio, a book caught my attention. The book was entitled, *Biblical Healing and Deliverance* by authors Chester & Betsy Kylstra.

The book prepared me for the dream, and it was through that dream the Holy Spirit revealed that I desperately needed healing. The authors were the creators of the 'Restoring the Foundations' healing, prayer and deliverance ministry and Dr. Butler was a trained facilitator. Along with others on her staff, she has been able to help so many through this healing and

2

anointed work.

Fear and deep roots of shame are two of the reasons it took me so long to write this book. I also had to make peace with my past before I could expose it to the world. Furthermore, I still struggled in some areas all while experiencing great deliverance in others. How could I write the book when my life story was still a work in progress? I wasn't famous, didn't have an entourage, no groupies, or any trappings of the wealthy life, at least not in dollars and cents. I didn't feel qualified or unique enough for my life's narrative to count, let alone expose my deepest darkest secrets. What I did know, despite everything, is I wanted to help others like myself to know they were not alone and they could overcome.

My story is a living testimony of deliverance and restoration. I went from a desolate and oppressed existence, to a higher place of loving and living although the odds would say otherwise. This book is for those who will open it and find some nuggets of truth that mirror their lives or the lives of someone they know. Hopefully they will find a solution, or have an AHA moment that will help them long after they close the covers.

Exposure of my sexual violations was long overdue, and many like me have tried to hide the shame instead of overcoming it. But then again, we were taught to 'hush up' about the predators who held hidden agendas in their heart. These predators used their sexual aggressions to violate and penetrate our innocent bodies and souls.

My first encounter with molestation was by a priest when I was in the third grade, and family members planted more seeds of violation.

The ultimate abuse came by the hands of my 34-year-old neighbor when I was 14 years old. That abuse involved emotional manipulation, rape and ultimately sexual control.

The results of enduring molestation, rape and sexual enslavement throughout my freshman year of high school changed my life in so many ways. It established roots of anger/bitterness, fear, failure, shame, unworthiness, desperation for true love, morbid obesity, lack of boundaries, inability to trust, awkwardness, self-sabotage, three failed marriages, an addiction to pornography and involvement in various sexual sins.

I was unable to relate to relationships in healthy ways. I did not understand the depth of the damage done to me by my neighbor at such a young age until years later. I kept trying to find normalcy without healing. For a long time, I was an angry and bitter person because I thought this was my portion in life and I hadn't signed on the dotted line for it. Where was that Cinderella ending for me?

I accepted Jesus Christ as my Lord and Savior in 1993, but

because of the abuses of my past, I struggled to accept Him and His leading in my life. I thought, "God only wants the 'good people,' not the jacked up people who have done yucky things to themselves and others.

The labels I placed on myself were deep and impactful, and consequently; when I became a new believer, *I wore the appearance of religion to cover my shame*. I wanted to make myself appear as having it all together before God and the congregation. They dressed and talked differently than I did. I believed this was the behavior of a Christian, and as long as I learned how to dress and speak right, God would be pleased with me.

I began to wear skirts to the floor and blouses up to my neck with minimal make-up; this was my idea of fitting in and appeasing a God who was impossible to please in my mind. I was so unhappy in the beginning of my Christian walk because of the false beliefs I held of how I perceived God to be. I was uncertain of what He was requiring of me to be in a right relationship with Him.

When I accepted Jesus Christ, He stood before God as my advocate, my defender and my intercessor. I would learn over time that He was sufficient before God as the sacrifice for my sins *(read Isaiah 53)*.

Imagine my surprise when I found out I was pre-destined to

be here, and God loved me first. He was already aware of where I had been, what I had done, as well as the things that had been done to me. The best part is that His plans for me and my life would supersede the past I had come to disdain.

> **Romans 8:29, 30** - *For those whom He foreknew [of whom He was aware and loved beforehand], He also destined from the beginning [foreordaining them] to be molded into the image of His Son {and share inwardly His likeness], that He might become the firstborn among many brethren.*
>
> *And those whom He thus ordained, He also called; and those whom He called, He also justified (acquitted, made righteous, putting them in right standing with Himself). And those whom He justified, He also glorified [raising them to a heavenly dignity and condition or state of being]* (AMP*).*

I give Jehovah God all the glory for being the potter of my existence long before I ever acknowledged Him. God has renamed me, restored me and re-birthed me in mass proportions; I now smile more days than I ever thought would be possible in my 59 years on the planet.

Living with regrets from a shameful past can set up generational scars. These scars will set roadblocks for generations to come until someone breaks the cycle and rewrites the family dialogue through the power of the Holy Spirit.

A Yucky Dialog is intended to encourage you wherever you find yourself right in this moment in time. Grab what you can from this story and share it with anyone, male or female, you know who may have been sexually violated on any level at any time.

I have met and spoken with men who were molested by other men and began to question their sexuality because of the violation. I noticed this especially if they didn't understand why their body responded to what they knew was wrong in their thoughts. To cover the confusion and shame, some of the men became players, whoremongers, pimps and so much more. They wanted to prove they were men instead of seeking help for the violations that were done to them.

I overcame and I am still overcoming with the love and acceptance of God. I was determined to see the assignment of victimization over my life canceled as I transitioned from victim to victorious living. I don't want you to stay stuck as long as I did: 38 years. Instead, I want you to know the hand of God's healing and blessings as soon as possible because you don't have time to waste.

I accepted the truth and cut ties with every untruth that the enemy used to try to keep me bound. How? By accepting Jesus Christ; I came to understand that He is the answer to every lie I had adopted as truth about God and myself because of what I had experienced. The enemy did not want me to ever gain the truth of the resurrection power of Jesus Christ. No matter how yucky (distasteful) my past has been, the love of the Father overcame my past before I ever hit the planet.

Are you ready? Let's do this!

Simply IvaB

Chapter One

Shattered to Be Remade[1]

Then I went down to the potter's house, and behold, he was working at the wheel. And the vessel that he was making from clay was spoiled in the hand of the potter; so, he made it over, reworking it into another vessel as it seemed good to the potter to make it.
Jeremiah 18:3-4 (AMP)

If you have ever dropped your favorite vase on the ground and watched it shatter into a zillion pieces, you know the feeling of being crippled with temporary disbelief. Your hand quickly flies to your mouth, and you stare at the irreparable damage, realizing it is like the last rites that you hear at the cemetery

---

[1] This chapter represents an update of work previously published in an anthology for women: Moore, Erika T. (2016). "From a Yucky Dialogue To a Promise". *Woman2Woman, "Let's Talk"*. MEP Publishing; Lillington, NC, pp. 95-113.

when they pronounce, "from ashes to ashes and dust to dust". Okay, maybe not as drastic, but you get the impact.

It is final, and there is no raising this vase back up to its former glory. No super glue or duct tape solution; it is gone forever. You walk slowly to the broom closet and grab your broom and dustpan and proceed to sweep up the shattered pieces to discard them in the trash.

For a brief time, you recall the vase and what it meant to your life. You try to remember where you got it from in the first place, how long you had it, and what you loved so much about it. Over time, you noticed a few new dings and scratches on the vase, but not enough to deem it irreversibly damaged with no further purpose. Many years ago, I had a conversation with God where I realized I was like that vase when God said, "Iva, I am going to shatter you and then remake you."

Shatter me? What could He mean by that? Thinking of those tiny shards of glass, I assumed it included pain and separation. The violations I experienced affected my spirit, soul and body. After being shattered, receiving my healing would involve revisiting painful memories, disappointments and failures. With the help of the Holy Spirit, I accepted this process for my deliverance.

Sometimes we become comfortable with our pain. Let me stop right here for a moment and let that sink in. When we have experienced a lot of pain, and it has become a part of us, how we think, how we act, what we say, and how we live our lives on a daily basis; we struggle to release the pain when it can no longer be our crutch for not moving on in life. We should always reach for the higher quality of life that Jesus Christ has promised us in *John 10:10*.

When God spoke of shattering to remake me, I was ready for the work that He wanted to do on the inside of me. I knew this meant I would no longer be able to stay in a negative, unhealed, dilapidating state of existence that led to seasons of emotional tantrums and brought unwanted attention. I knew this process would be painful because it meant I had to finally grow up and live my life the way God intended, which was victorious and without the excuse of victimization. It would also challenge me to learn to trust God (*read Proverbs 3: 5-6*).

The God of creation who also created me in the womb of my mother by the seed of my father was going to shatter me, and when He finished, He was then going to remake me? He began to explain to help me understand the process I was about to enter. He spoke as a potter who had created a vessel that he molded into a thing of beauty. As I was created by His masterful hands, He created what pleased Him.

> *Psalm 139:14 - I will praise You, for I am fearfully and wonderfully made; Marvelous are Your works, And that my soul knows very well (NIV).*

Psalm 139:17 - How precious also are Your thoughts to me, O God! How vast is the sum of them! If I could count them, they would outnumber the sand. When I awake, I am still with You (NIV).

Once I was finished being created in His heart, He released me to Earth for the very purpose that He intended. My life story began to unfold in the home of my earthly father, Raymond Thomas 'Rocky' Brassfield, and my mother, Lucy Thelma Brassfield. I was the new baby to two older siblings, Nep and Chay, and this was our family at the starting block of my existence on December 2, 1958.

Around the second grade, my parents divorced because my father struggled with deep roots of anger. I believe this anger stemmed from the loss of his mother who died at the young age of 22, followed by his father's death at the age of 26 just four years later. As a result of the loss of both his parents, he and his siblings were placed in an orphanage and the foster care system.

My father's anger manifested and he would release bouts of physical abuse on my mother and would torment my big brother. Eventually, my mother had enough of this often times explosive environment and moved us out. I was too young to recall a lot about that time; I assumed my role as the baby of the family and adjusted as such.

One day in the third grade my sister Chay and I were

running home from school as we had done on many occasions, but something was frighteningly different about our run. I ran for a short distance and had to keep stopping to catch my breath while my sister yelled at me to hurry up. A two-block journey felt like a five-mile marathon in my little chest. That evening I ended up in the hospital and the diagnosis was asthma. My father also had asthma, but I was the only child out of the three of us who would struggle with it for a long time to come.

The first night in the hospital I was placed inside of an enormous oxygen tent that covered the whole bed. (We have come a long way with treatments since that time.) My parents went home and released me to the care of the doctors and nurses at a hospital in Toledo, Ohio. They did not know that lurking in the shadows under a religious cloak was a predator. That night, one of the hospital priests entered my room and proceeded to touch me inappropriately and then slithered back out of the room. I never told a soul until later in my adult life.

When God explained the need to shatter and remake me as His vessel, He helped me to understand that incidences like the violation by the priest became a ding on my vessel. I struggled for a long time with the burden of this secret and I didn't know if it was something I had done wrong or if there was something about me that let the priest think he had the right to violate me.

I came to understand that it wasn't my fault, but I still

carried the secret and the shame. The shame only grew stronger over the next several years as I experienced more violations to my body and soul. The dings on my vessel were growing.

By fifth grade, my mother married a man named Ivan George Osbourne who would become a dad in my heart because of the similarities of our names. He was of Jamaican descent and knew how to build and fix anything. No matter what he did, I wanted to watch and learn because he had creative life skills.

My natural father was still very active in my life, but his life also involved two other wives and two other daughters. The lives of my parents continued even though we were no longer a family unit. Sometimes as children, we forget that our parents still have relational desires and needs. My father still spent time with me and had an active role in my life while he also tried to create a new family unit with a second wife and later with a third wife, with whom he fathered two more daughters. I never felt neglected or abandoned because of these changes in his life, and I embraced my two new little sisters Tori and Ashley.

Fifth grade brought a new neighborhood and a new school. I did not adjust well; I was a social misfit, and from the moment I started going to elementary school, I was getting beat up all of the time.

On the third day of school when the day had ended, a girl

took my head and slammed it into the school building until I began to bleed. She gave no reason and I never asked; I didn't even know the girl. The three o'clock hour after school became my time to run like hell! I wanted to get home because schoolyard fights were constant. As the new girl, I was a prime target for many bullies. A new type of violation was manifesting which created new dents on my vessel. I was now officially a victim and being victimized at every turn.

I had behavioral problems in school, and I remember being sent to an educational counselor many times between the fifth and eighth grades. My mother worked, but had to come to the school constantly due to my disruptions and conflicts. My older siblings went to different schools, so I was left on my own to survive. I didn't know how to fight, so I ran. Now and then, I targeted a weaker girl and beat her up on the way home.

I would disrobe her while fighting so she would be exposed. I wanted to humiliate her, but I was too young to understand the significance of that action at the time. Later I came to understand that just as I was disrobed and violated sexually in the past by others, I demonstrated the same disrobing and mishandling of this girl who I considered to be weak as I fought her.

I saw myself as weak, so I allowed attention to be drawn to her weakness in order to paralyze her from fighting me back as I attacked her. I thought I could take the focus off myself as a victim, but it didn't work because I was still full of fear.

By the eighth grade I grew tired of four years of being in fights. One day another match was scheduled at the three o'clock hour; some girl wanted to fight me because she saw me as weak. So here we go again, except this time something in me stepped up, and I decided to fight back with all that was in me. I fought back and won the fight! I'd found a new sense of fearlessness.

The girl challenged me to another dual the next day, and I whipped her again and never had to fight again. It was amazing that when I stood up, faced my fear and fought back, my enemies were defeated and pushed back for good. I also lost the urge to pick on weaker girls after that. I wasn't a victim anymore and didn't need to create other victims to fill the void.

I experienced a victory on one front, while brewing on another front was a life changing, chain of events. These events would add more scratches to my vessel. During the summer of my eighth-grade year, I began to hang around a house in my neighborhood that belonged to a 34 year old, single man who often worked in his garage. To this day I still wonder how I was ever alone with this man; I must have developed some sense of trust, and I was always too curious for my own good.

I found myself hanging out more in his garage while he worked. One day he offered me a beer, and it made me feel a little grown. Next, he introduced me to smoking cigarettes. Feeling a little more trusting and grown, I continued to spend more time with this man that I will call Joe.

I cannot recall the type of conversations between us; I just remember more exposure to adult-type things. I was invited into his home after watching him work on remodeling his garage many times, and an adult/child connection began to evolve.

I was fourteen years old and still naïve; Joe started to treat me like an adult and began to watch me around boys my age. My identity became distorted, as I could no longer fit in easily with the kids my own age. I was still too young to fit in with the adults, although I was entertaining adult thoughts and actions. The boundaries inside of me had already been violated by molestations, and the enemy was setting a trap for the kill.

We lived across the alley from Joe. I had a clear view of his home from our upstairs bathroom, so I spent time obsessing over what he was doing. Even though Joe introduced me to pornography, he still had not touched me physically. Up until this time, even though I'd been molested, I was still a virgin. His seduction was slow and steady; it was first emotional and then physical. Between being given a key to his home, beer, cigarettes, access to porn, and freedom to come and go as I pleased; I was a young girl moving way before her time.

The summer of my eighth-grade year was the summer of my

undoing with Joe. I had been out at a party with kids my age when I stopped by his house on the way back home. That night, I came through the back door using my key and he was angry. I could smell the sour scent of beer on his breath. "Where have you been?" he asked, his voice was close to a growl. "I was at a party with some friends. It was no big deal," I stated. "You're lying," he said. He pulled back his hand and slapped me across the face. He hit me several more times and mumbled, "I'm not playing games with you anymore."

I was scared. I had never seen him like this. Joe had always been easy-going toward me and had never once raised his voice at me or been displeased with me. I didn't know what to do. I certainly didn't know what to do when he started to take my clothes off. That night, at the hands of this man I was no longer a virgin. Everything inside of me was awakened as a young girl playing an adult role. This man created a climate in his home for sexual enslavement. I was his sexual property and he did everything within his power to make sure he was the only person to have access to me for a year, and I was not the same again.

My distorted view of relationships and love was a by-product of this season of my young life. This was not a mere ding on my vessel, this was a gouge that went through to the core of my soul.

At the end of that summer and the beginning of my

freshmen year, boys my age became merely toys in my warped mind because of my continued involvement with Joe. He would give me fifty-dollar bills for lunch, but I never understood the connection money had to our secrets until later in life. A prostitute is paid in exchange for sexual favors; Joe would give me money as a form of placating me or keeping me quiet.

As a young girl, two things were going on with me at the time. First, I did not tell anyone about Joe because I liked having money to spend; what young person doesn't? The second thing is that once I was no longer a virgin, I was awakened to sexual desires and I responded to those desires by continuing to return to Joe's home. I did not expose what was going on between us. I knew that Joe would have been sent to prison if it was revealed, and like many victims I became protective of him in this situation that was a crime.

Daily he would leave his job, drive out to my school and park out of the sight of teachers to take me home. He didn't want me riding the school bus with the boys my age; he was very possessive. In his sadistic mind, he saw himself in a relationship with me, no matter how forbidden. Of course, what is done in the dark can only stay hidden for so long.

My parents had their bedroom and bathroom downstairs in our house. My brother, sister, and I had our bedrooms upstairs with our shared bathroom. I concocted the idea to sneak downstairs in the middle of the night, under the premise of getting a glass of water, so I could sneak out of the house and across the alley to Joe's house since I had a key. I would quietly open the basement door, tiptoe down the stairs, and sneak out of a window. Then, I would sneak back home before sunrise.

I got away with this for quite some time, until one morning the basement door to the kitchen was locked and I couldn't get back in. I knew the jig was up and my mother was waiting, but I still never volunteered information about Joe. I found out later that she had become suspicious of something someone in the neighborhood had said. During that time, communities were the village and folks looked out for each other's children. She would not get the full story about Joe until I was grown and had children of my own.

The thing that broke the cycle of destructive behavior with Joe came at the beginning of my sophomore year. We bought a new house on the other side of town and the move took me entirely away from Joe. I started going to a new high school, and I was too far away from Joe to see him, but his scent and presence were still all over me. Everything he taught me, I used to my advantage with boys.

During high school, I became very promiscuous. I knew one language in relationships, and that was sex; I didn't know any other way. Girls like me wore labels such as fast, slutty, around-the-way girl and good time girl. I knew the art of seduction, and I used it in every way. Emotionally, I knew no boundaries because the lines had already been crossed. I only knew lust and passion and the dings on my vessel became so numerous that only God knew the full extent.

When I was around twelve years old, my mother discovered I had a voice to sing so she placed me with Lola Smith, a vocal coach. I began to sing publicly with the Lola Smith All-Stars. We sang in nursing homes, at the state hospital (where my dad used to stay on occasion) for mentally ill patients, and anywhere we could command an audience. Singing became a huge part of my life and it became my rope of survival because I could escape not being a typical teenage girl, which was the pain of my existence. I would bring people to tears and receive standing ovations when I sang from the broken places within my heart.

I started entering beauty pageants around that time and won several titles. I also became a runway model for several of the department stores in the city. When I was on stage I could escape, while off-stage I shrank back to my secret pleasures and shame. My high school life was an existence of obscurity, and it was also during my junior year in high school that I suddenly lost my daddy Rocky at the young age of 42. He passed away on my step-father's birthday, February 23, 1975; it was devastating for me.

Coming up in our home, we briefly went to church. When my parents were still together, we went to a Black Baptist church. When they split up, we went to a White Baptist church.

From there, my mother began to seek after God through different avenues. Throughout high school, it was Transcendental Meditation, Spiritualistic churches where psychics gave you readings, New Age, The Secret Rosicrucian Society and other false religions that became my foundation to God. This only added to my confusion and a whole lot more dents on my vessel.

During my last year of high school, I won a four-year scholarship to Cincinnati Conservatory of Music as a soprano opera major. Before I left home, I entered a local competition of Miss Black and Gold by the Alpha Phi Alpha Fraternity. The pageant brought in a host of hairdressers from a local hair salon. The stylist who chose to do my hair was unique; this young man was tall, dark, and handsome. I remember his engaging smile and him saying, "I choose you". Of course, I was smitten. He and I were the same age and yet something was so different about him compared to other boys our age.

Once again, I won the competition and received a standing ovation. I also won the opportunity to compete in the district-wide competition later that year. After the competition, the hairdresser and I agreed to stay in touch while I was away at college.

Once in college, my lack of preparation was evident in my studies, and I struggled to keep up. All I ever wanted to do was sing, nothing else. Learning music theory was the farthest thing from my mind, not realizing how necessary it would be if I were to further my music studies. I wanted to be a world-renowned opera singer, such as the likes of Leontyne Price and Kathleen Battle who were my favorites. I desired to sing in the Sydney Opera House of Australia and perform on the stage of Carnegie Hall in New York City. I wanted to be like Diana Ross in the movie, *Lady Sings the Blues*. I knew the entire song repertoire from that movie because the songs were full of pain.

Billie Holiday was a legendary jazz singer that the movie, *Lady Sings the Blues* was based upon. She was a phenomenal singer who met with some negative circumstances in her life. Rape, prostitution and drug addiction stifled her greatest singing potential. She was always on the edge of a breakthrough, only to meet with opposition that would fight against her highest potential to succeed.

I related to her story as a teenager. She sang songs such as "Good Morning Heartache" which were the public wailings of her private pain. I grabbed hold of these songs because I was in sadness and grief. I felt heartache in the mornings I woke in the arms of a male who cared nothing for me or I for him. I'd become depleted of expectation of anything more than a sexual encounter.

The hairdresser started writing me while I was away in college, and sent me books about his religion. I learned he was a Jehovah's Witness and then understood why he was so different from all the rest of the boys and men I had been exposed to. He was a gentleman to me; a kind soul who never tried to take physical advantage of me, and I wasn't sure how to respond to him. It was a foreign language to my flesh as I began to read the books and started asking questions.

I started making more frequent trips home, and we started dating. For the first time since the age of 14, and now at the age of 19, I was celibate with a man. He brought honor to me in a way I had never known. Unfortunately, there was a battle between him and some of his family members. They made it plain that I was a worldly girl and not good enough for him. He made his stand for me, and we were married January of 1978. I was 20 years old and quit college to become his wife and a Jehovah's Witness. A year later, I became pregnant with our daughter Candace, who became our world.

I felt like my life had taken a turn for the better. I found God through religion and a husband to die for; he loved me and cared for me, but I still struggled with where I had come from. Without deliverance from the roots of my past, I was always tiptoeing back to skirt with temptation. Just a few short years into the marriage, I committed adultery and then shared it with my husband and eventually the Board of Elders, at the Kingdom Hall.

At 22 years old, I did not fully understand the repercussions of my infidelity in my marriage and to the religious organization.

The marriage did not survive the betrayal, and I fled the home due to his physical abuse in front of our daughter. My necessary escape ultimately led to a season being homeless. When I fled, I left everything behind. My daughter Candace and I lived in several different places at the mercy of others with only our clothes.

During this time of separation, I became pregnant with my second daughter by someone I knew from high school. It was a one-night stand and, although we never embarked on a relationship, we agreed to raise our daughter. This sealed the fate of my marriage as irreconcilable because I would never consider an abortion. I had one in my senior year of high school and made up my mind I would never have another. I would also never expect my estranged husband to raise another man's child.

I had made a complete mess of my life, and my vessel went from dings to gashes by then. I was dis-fellowshipped from the organization of Jehovah's Witnesses and told not to pray because Jehovah God would not hear me since I was a sinner. As a result of being told that, I went into eleven years of spiritual limbo; but all the while God was watching out for me. My friend Toni, a born-again believer, began sowing seeds of truth about Jesus Christ every chance she had. I believed the elders of Jehovah's Witnesses when they said God would not hear my prayers. I was ashamed of my life choices up until that time, but God knew better and so did Toni.

After my second daughter, Giavanna (Gigi) was born, I settled into being a single mother with no life skills. I was trying to raise two daughters by myself and had the mentality of a child. I was still homeless and living on welfare when an acquaintance helped me secure a place to live for my growing family. This would be my first place since previously I left my parents home when I got married and moved with my husband. I had never lived on my own, so I was being challenged to grow up quickly because two little girls were depending on me.

Even though I had been previously married, I was underdeveloped as a woman. I lacked the maturity and healing to function on a more grounded level. Because of all that happened with Joe and the aftermath, and after what I had done to my ex-husband, I took on self-hatred and a degree of degradation. I punished myself through the men I engaged with and became a victim of my sins and sinful choices. As far as I was concerned, God saw me the same exact way.

My belief system concerning God was tainted with false myths and beliefs about who He was as God. I thought He had created this long list of all my sins and failures and was keeping me at bay until I could atone for them all. How sad of a commentary when we don't know the truth about how much God truly does love us. He loves us so much that He gave His only begotten son as the only atonement for our sins (**John 3:16**). God is not mad at us for the things we have experienced and gone through even if it was our fault.

In 1985, Joyce, one of my best friends, dragged me to the unemployment office, and we put in applications for the three factories in our city: Ford, Jeep, and Hydramatic (GM). Three weeks later, I got a phone call from Hydramatic and went to work in the factory.

My work experiences up until that time centered around office work such as secretarial duties or as a receptionist. The factory would prove to be a greater challenge than I expected when I started in 1985. The great part of it was that I was able to get off welfare, move my little family to better housing, and start on the road to taking responsibility for my family even if it had nothing to do with singing.

A few years later I met and married my next husband. I wanted to try and recapture what I had lost in my first marriage. I knew the day that I married my second husband I was making a terrible mistake. He was a great person, but struggled with addictions to alcohol and drugs. I woke up that morning and took my daughters to school, then threw a hat on my head, tucked my nightgown into my jeans, and we went downtown to the justice of the peace and got married.

After that we went to the jewelry store and purchased a set of wedding rings for the both of us and then we hit the time clock at GM because we didn't have any money to celebrate. I called my mom later that day to tell her the news, and then I called the doctor. I had broken out in hives all over my body.

Right after we married, the childhood asthma I thought I had left behind returned. I knew I had made a colossal mistake and that feeling manifested physically.

I turned thirty and we had been living together all of thirteen months. It was then I realized I was still making lousy choices where men were concerned. I was addicted to the Cinderella kind of love, which I had a small taste of and subsequently lost in my first marriage. Eighteen months into this union, I divorced him due to his alcohol and drug addiction that I could not tolerate anymore.

I was always trying to heal everyone else but never sought healing for myself. Everyone else's healing and liberation gave me a sense of purpose for doing good, so their healing remained a priority over my own. I felt like the better I did for others, the better chance I had of winning brownie points with God; and maybe He would give me a pass on my past.

I now felt more shame for having been married and divorced twice by the age of thirty-one. The asthma was starting to send me to the hospital for extended periods of time, and my mother came to visit me in the hospital frequently and every time she was more and more worried. Not just about my health, but about my life in general. I remember my mother asking me, "What are you doing in this relationship?"

I was with someone new who had the same drug addictions

as my last husband, and I was repeating patterns. "I'm going to learn what I need to about this unhealthy connection," I said to my mother while lying in my hospital bed. I finally turned my thoughts to God after all those years of being a dis-fellowshipped Jehovah's Witness.

I gave my best attempt at a prayer that day. I spoke to God about the generational bloodline curses that I believed existed. I had been molested, raped, and I was scared my daughters were on the same path. I did not know they had already been violated by people I thought I could trust.

I knew I would have grandchildren one day and I prayed that I would be a praying granny for them. It would be some time before that prayer in the hospital bed would begin to be answered. To date I have five beautiful grandchildren who motivate and inspire me to walk with God daily as an example for them. As long as I am alive, one of my most significant goals is to present The Gospel to my grandchildren by the way I live my life. I desire to help them grow into the knowledge of God. The heart of my prayer is that not one of them will be lost to this world; Legaci, Akil Jr., London, Heiress and King will be born-again believers.

From 1992 to 1993, two significant things happened in my life: I met and married another man, and I became a born-again believer in Jesus Christ. I met this husband-to-be while on my job. I was somewhat resistant since I already had one failed marriage connected to my workplace, but I allowed a crack into the closed door of my heart. He was funny and unashamed to be seen with me in public. Before him, I did not place a high demand on the men I encountered because of my lack of confidence and fear of rejection. I got nothing outside of sex.

This man went past the surface of my existence and for the first time in a very long time, he saw something in me. Most of my relationships with men were void of depth. No wining or dining, no plays, no dancing, and no exotic trips to foreign places. He was different. He engaged me outside of the safety of my walls at home and introduced me to life on another level. I was excited for this change, as were my children, who watched me withdraw from life on so many levels for years due to asthma and depression.

To celebrate my birthday in December of 1992, I went on my first cruise to the Bahamas. I was scared and thrilled–at the same time. While there, I discovered something; God had to exist for such a beautiful place to exist! The more beauty of the island that I experienced, the more I wanted to know the God who created it.

As I was considering a relationship with God after years of being a dis-fellowshipped Jehovah's Witness, it was essential to know who God was past the rules and regulations of organized religion. I needed to know Him past the judgments that men placed on me. I wanted to know Him on a personal level, which was something I had yet to experience.

I laid out one sunny afternoon with the balmy breezes of a December wind at about 82-degrees with my eyes closed and breathing better than I had in a very long time. I told God I needed to know who he was. When I returned home I felt refreshed and rejuvenated with a new purpose.

On New Year's Eve, I told my then boyfriend I would not be going to the cabaret that night. I wanted to bring in the New Year at church, so we went hunting for a church to attend. The first one was packed with standing room only, so we found a different one and I began my transitional spiritual journey that night.

I started to go to church on a regular basis after praying about whether I should go back to the Kingdom Hall of Jehovah's Witnesses or a church. I felt a pull to the church and attended a non-denominational church in Toledo, Ohio. I had been attending that church on a regular basis for a couple of months, before I surrendered my life to becoming a born-again believer.

The afternoon of March 3, 1993, I was watching a Christian program while preparing to go to work. I received a call from a young lady who had been a babysitter for my girls when they were young. She had also been sowing seeds into my heart to come to Jesus, and that afternoon she asked, "Have you received Jesus as your Lord and Savior?" Suddenly the phone went dead, and all I could hear was the television as a TV Evangelist began leading people to Christ. I got on my knees right then and there and asked God to forgive me of all my sins. I invited Jesus Christ into my heart as my personal Lord and Savior according to *Romans 10:9*, *"because if you acknowledge and confess with your mouth that Jesus is Lord [recognizing His power, authority, and majesty as God], and believe in your heart that God raised Him from the dead, you will be saved" (AMP).*

The night before this, I had been smoking heavily and worrying about where my life was headed. I heard an audible voice say, "Trust in the Lord with all your heart." I knew the scripture well from, *Proverbs 3:5-6 which says, "Trust in the Lord with all thine heart; and lean not unto thine understanding. In all your ways acknowledge Him and He shall direct your path"(KJV).*

All night I had sensed that something was about to happen that was not going to be normal, but didn't know what. I was scared. In my heart, I felt that I needed to break up with my boyfriend. I'd been growing tired of the way he treated me, and I knew I deserved better, so I wrote him a letter.

I saw him after getting to work the day I accepted Christ and, before he could respond to my goodbye letter, I shared with him that I became born-again that afternoon. As I talked, I felt a tightening in my chest. The chain-smoking from the night before had exacerbated my asthma and it felt like my chest was going to explode. My boss had to call an ambulance to transport me to the hospital.

My boyfriend was going to ride to the hospital with me, but his boss said "no", and later we found out that was a blessing in disguise for him. Instead he went off to the chapel at work on his break, planning to arrive at the hospital shortly. I was strapped onto the gurney and loaded into the ambulance.

As we left the GM plant, I heard a voice say, "This ambulance is going to crash with you in it." I was too stunned to do anything, but shortly after I heard the driver cry out and I knew we were crashing. I cried out in defiance, "Jehovah, no! I am not leaving like this." It was as if the whole ambulance went around my body until it came to rest on its side. The paramedic attending to me was upside down and blood seeped from a wound on her head.

When the doors opened, I was in the back sitting upright strapped to the gurney without one scratch. I was in a daze as the realization came to me of what I had just experienced. On the very day that I had received Jesus Christ into my heart as my personal Lord and Savior, the enemy tried to kill me.

I was reluctantly transported to the hospital in another ambulance. My boyfriend was waiting at the hospital when I arrived. Having passed the accident on the way, he did not believe that I could've been in there. It became a defining moment for him as well, and the next day we went to Bible study at the church where he gave his life to Christ.

Now that we were both born-again believers, we did not want to be in sin, so we decided to get married. We did not consult God about this decision and it would prove to be another disastrous mistake for my girls and me. Within six months of the marriage, it was revealed that he was molesting my youngest daughter. When he tried to go after my oldest daughter one night, she bravely exposed him. The resulting devastation and fall out was harsh.

Without revealing every detail, we separated and sought counseling. As a mother, all I could swallow at the time was that I had failed to protect my daughters from what I had gone through, and that I had brought a predator right under my roof for the sake of having someone in my life, and hadn't see it coming.

I never allowed him around my daughters again, but instead I tried to believe for his deliverance and the saving of my marriage because I didn't want to face another failed marriage. Coming from a background of dysfunction with men, I wanted more than anything to feel normal. Having a successful marriage was extremely important to me because I always wanted a family. My parents had five broken marriages between them: my father had three, my mother had two, and I did not want the same for myself. This marriage would represent my third failure at making a successful relationship work. This would take the biggest chunk out of my vessel.

For the next seven years we lived together and apart until I finally let it go. There was nothing left to fight for; I had decided that the verbal, emotional and physical fighting had to end. When it was over, my self-esteem was out the door and I didn't have much else to go on. It was somewhere in the process of this epic battle during my marriage that God spoke to me and said he was going to shatter me to re-make me.

All the violations, no matter how big or small defined how I saw myself and how I responded to life. There were 'nicks' and 'dings' in my life that had to be shattered. To merely break me would mean I could be super-glued back together, but to shatter me would shatter the nicks and dings to an unrecognizable place and I could not be put back together the same way ever again. God's process to shatter me and then re-make me began the process He had for my healing and deliverance from the sexual violations of my past.

The potter in *Jeremiah 18:3-4* had the power and ability to keep the substance of the marred vessel and place it once again on the potter's wheel in order to recreate and mold it all over again. He didn't need new clay, but he had the masterful skills to use the same clay, and make it pliable in his hands for his purpose all over again. God wanted to take all the things I had gone through and make me a new creation in Christ Jesus. The former things that infected my life as a disease could now pass away. I could now be re-made in His glory for such a time as this.

> **2 Corinthians 5:17** *Therefore if any person is [in grafted] in Christ (the Messiah) he is a new creation (a new creation altogether); the old [previous moral and spiritual condition] has passed away. Behold, the fresh and new has come! (AMP)*

What a beautiful promise from the Lord. Even though the process would be painful at times, I knew God had a plan for deliverance and growth that would far exceed my pain. He has not failed in restoring much of my life that was lost through molestation and rape. Peace does prevail!

Chapter Two

What Is Your Name?

Recovering Your Lost Identity

For years I knew God had set me apart for a work, but I battled with believing I was anointed to do it. It had been confirmed many times, yet my insecurities and shame would void those words spoken over my life.

The year was 1999, and I was going through the last separated period from my third husband among other things. I was attending a Prophetic Training seminar. My spiritual state was fragile but determined. Some of the women in our ministry attended the same seminar. Every one of them was confirmed in some area of ministry except for me.

That Friday night, Nina-Marie Leslie who was the seminar facilitator taught us, and then prophesied to many in attendance. I longed for a word of confirmation from the Lord so desperately, but it never happened. The prophetic words that had been spoken into my life up until that time had not yet come to pass.

I was in a fragile spiritual state with a marriage that was crumbling before my eyes, I had my hands full trying to help my children who had also been violated by my husband, and fighting health issues that were trying to literally take my life. At my church, I had grown tired of dealing with a body of leaders who I did not trust anymore. I needed God to tell me that there was still purpose for me to do one day, because I saw no evidence that presented such a case.

Saturday morning we gathered in that church once again, full and filled with anticipation. I was seated with a group from my church about two rows from the front while Nina-Marie was teaching. She began to prophesy to me, and it took a moment before I realized she was actually speaking to me.

She had me to stand up, and she began to minister to me in such a healing way. She confirmed the calling of God upon my life. She acknowledged that I had experienced so many pot shots in the spirit that I didn't think I was anointed. She affirmed that I was the woman for the job and no one else could do what I was called to do, so I needed to lace up my Reeboks and run the race set before me. She sent me to the feet of the Pastor of that house where I kneeled, and she laid hands on me and prayed over me for strength.

Of course, I was a hot mess by then, but confirmation had come. Finally, Nina-Marie turned to the rest of the people sensing they were ready for more personal prophetic impartation. She spoke and said she had come strictly that day for me. I was the only one she would prophesy over in that morning session. I was floored by the favor of God toward me that day through his servant, and I felt great peace the rest of the day.

Of course, it wasn't long before the enemy came and tried to rip that word away from me. He used those in leadership who I should have been able to trust. It was after that encounter, a recent dream about the word I received from Nina-Marie was brought back to my remembrance. I'd had that dream a few weeks before the seminar and it became a landmark of confirmation for me as well.

About a year later, my pastors set a date for my first sermon as May 28, 2000. I had been teaching bible studies and had delivered Sunday school messages from the time I became a born-again believer, but this moment was a different position of ministry. I stepped into that moment without ever going through healing and deliverance or counseling because of my shameful past.

I thought I was ready for ministry without wholeness, and I didn't see the trials that would follow my decision to leap into ministry without healing. It would be another fifteen years before I was ready to receive the processing of ministry as I was licensed and ordained on April 26, 2015, finally healed and delivered from the shame of my past.

It was an afternoon service and family, co-workers, church family and friends showed up in support. I was surprised to see how many were in attendance and I was most proud because my mom was sitting in the front row.

I ministered out of **Matthew 11:28-30**. When I was done, Deb, one of my dearest friends who had been supporting me, pulled me aside and said that, "the Holy Spirit has a warning, and there is a great temptation coming your way" now that I had stepped into the position of making a public declaration of ministry. She shared the alarm and it began to roll in my spirit. I didn't understand the impact of what was coming until it was upon me.

Once home I reflected on the events that had just transpired in my life that Sunday afternoon. The prayers from leadership and hands were laid upon me as each person spoke into my life. The consensus was that I was called to minister to marriages, families and women. Those areas are where my passion in helping others had always been.

It didn't make sense to me that I would be called to the ministry of marriage, families, relationships and women when those were areas of my greatest personal failures. I wondered how I could be called to what I have not been able to conquer.

Remember, I was facing my third failure at marriage during this time. I cried out to God, "Lord, I heard from the leadership on today, but what do You say about what You called me to do?"

I didn't even get the prayer out good when I received a phone call from a young wife. She was about to leave her husband due to his addiction to pornography and some other things. Because pornography was an area of addiction for me in my past, I could minister on that stronghold in her husband, and reassure her that she was doing nothing wrong. She had become weary and was losing faith. I ministered to her, then prayed for her and hung up the phone. The Lord asked me, "was that confirmation enough." In the midst of my own failed third marriage, I had to minister to someone else concerning her marriage.

Sharing so many of my failures and shame in this book has not been easy, but I wanted to make the sacrifice so others may know the same freedom in their life no matter what caused their private shame. My appetite always involved men; my life sabotages engaged men, and my identity was connected to the acceptance or rejection of men. It was what I knew and lived from the age of 14, and it was also what I thought was behind me.

I never wanted to be single and saved. I wanted to be married because of the passions of my flesh, my need to feel love whether that love was real or false, and my desire to have my own family. I married my last husband against all the signs and hesitations not to. Lust was our motivation while we clashed on everything necessary to build a stable Christian marriage. As I stated before *I never asked God if we should marry, I did what I thought was best for my survival in my new walk as a born-again believer.*

> *Proverbs 12:15* - *The way of the* [arrogant] *fool* [who rejects God's wisdom] *is right in his own eyes, But a wise and prudent man is he who listens to counsel (AMP).*

Praying to God concerning your life partner is exceptionally vital, I can't stress this enough. If you're sexually active with this person before marriage, you have opened the door to a soul tie, and are unable to discern whether this was God's plan for you or not. Your discernment is now cloudy.

I thought my marriage would be a safety net for my struggles with pornography, lust, and the fear of being alone. I married a man with whom the only thing we had in common was a vibrant and very active sex life. A great sex life does not equate to a stable marriage. As I look back over it now, I was very selfish and fleshly in my reasons for marrying this particular man. My choice was costly not only to me, but also my daughters.

My lack of deliverance from the *roots* of my past were lying dormant waiting for their time to be exposed. It is a mistake for all parties involved when we try to hide in relationships without deliverance. I entered and operated in this marriage out of my broken place with my broken expectations, and the marriage suffered from the beginning. I was a new born-again believer in a new marriage, and I thought that was sufficient.

Satan, your enemy, is against any progress in your life on any level. He loves it when we try and hide our sins or try to function with them in our walk with God. God desires that we acknowledge our sins, repent and turn away from them. He wants us to allow Him to help us dig for those roots and destroy them. I tried to avoid the process of cleansing and growth by being married. I learned that I still had to walk the process out when the marriage ended eight years later, and I was single again. I accepted my failure in this marriage and walked away as God confirmed my release from the union. I was 42 years old and now divorced for the third time.

While writing this book, the revelation of repeated family patterns was unveiled to me. By the age of 42, my father had already been married three times; at the time of my father's untimely death, he was preparing to divorce his third wife, but never made it to the court appointment. Like my father, my third marriage ended at 42 years of age. It would be 18 years after that marriage ended that I would understand the generational connection to my marriages and divorces. This knowledge also helped me as my oldest daughter Candace planned her wedding, because my greatest desire for them is that they succeed in their marriage.

The Holy Spirit revealed that the curse of divorce in our bloodline would never come neigh the dwelling of this new union. When my daughter Candace got engaged, it was one of the happiest moments for me as a mom. God had already revealed to me that He ordained their marriage.

Today, they are growing stronger at 19 years and counting! They are the parents of my oldest two grandchildren and God has placed His hand upon them. They have worked hard and are writing a new family script on marriage. God is good!

Many times, we look with our natural eyes as a point of clarity when we receive warnings about circumstances that involve us. My friend Deb warned me that a great temptation was coming my way, but because I was married, even though we were at the end; I never thought that temptation would involve a man. I rested in the security of my broken marriage.

I learned that every experience is different, so we cannot judge current situations entirely by every past experience. If we are not careful, we can potentially miss the enemy coming with a twist because we failed to ask the Holy Spirit to sharpen our discernment. Our spiritual eyes must be 20/20 and our spiritual ears clear of all wax.

Now back to the great temptation I had been warned about. It was now upon me. He was older, mature and very respectful to me. He was more like a father-type, a protector and never crass in his conversation as were so many others. He was also married. We started an affair that would last for the next six years. I turned from God and went back to what was familiar to me. There were also a couple of other yucky situations that I became involved in as well. I tried to live two different lives with one foot in the things of God and one foot in the world, which was a formula for total crazy and did not work at all.

I was ashamed of how I was living and felt trapped by the roots of my past. After those six years of emptiness, I went on a fast to repent and turn my way back to God. I stopped the relationship with this man and finally started on the long road to healing. I committed to never being involved with a married man again after following this path many times in my past. I remember two significant moments from the Lord during this time.

The first came after the divorce was final in my third marriage, as I began a mission to find my next husband. After making a commitment to never be entangled with a married man again, I began focusing attention on someone I worked with who was single. One day while walking through the job, I heard as clear as day, "until I have your heart there will not be another." I knew my Heavenly Father was trying to save me the time, effort and heartache of running into new relationships, so that deliverance and healing could finally begin. Another man or rushed marriage would never be the solution to the broken places in my life.

I was hard-headed, and not ready to surrender this area of my life. I ignored what I heard from God and kept trying to meet someone without first changing anything on the inside of me. I wanted to marry again, and the sooner the better. I zoomed in all my efforts toward this specific co-worker, and became involved in a connection that would take me a couple more years to untangle. Spiritually, I was weak, yet still crying out for deliverance.

I was determined to keep full control over this area of my life, especially away from God. My identity was rooted in getting and keeping a man. I was taught this from my experience with Joe at fourteen, so in my mind, to take that away meant that I would be lost.

I didn't want God involved because I felt that He would take away my dependence on men, my comfortable place, away from me. If He did that, I felt I would crumble and experience extreme loneliness and feelings of rejection. I needed to control the thing that made me feel like I was somebody. It would be later in life, after my deliverance, when I would finally understand I was never in control of this area anyway.

The truth is that you cannot control another person. I

learned that I couldn't force men to love me, I couldn't buy their love, and I couldn't hold them captive with sex (which is such a temporary fix). They will only be there as long as they want to be there.

I found myself back doing the same destructive habits I lived by before becoming a born-again believer. Now, I was backslidden. The second significant moment happened while sharing a break with this guy, outside at work, and making plans to be with him after work. He left to go to the restroom as I was enjoying the beautiful night's breeze and my thoughts about being with him later. Then suddenly, just as when a news station displays BREAKING NEWS, an alert plowed right into my thoughts. My Father in Heaven had a precise and clear message for me. I wrote that message in my journal and will share it here.

October 3, 2003, Friday, 2:49 am - *Words from the Lord:*
No man could ever understand you or know you as I do, because I knew you before you were ever created in your mother's womb. I know your needs, wants and desires. Sex is not love and what I have for you is greater. The one I am preparing for you will have my heart for you. You are enveloped in my love. It is all around you. (of course, I am balling by now because I had never heard anything like this before).

Those words from my Lord touched my heart in a special way. They were the most loving and precious things I had ever heard. Then I heard it again, "The one I have for you will have my heart for you." It was a defining moment, but my soulish thoughts just wanted to know when, where and who. When was this man coming? Where was he? Who was the man God had for me who would carry His heart for me?

It would be several more years of wasting time trying to make things in this area of my life the way I wanted them to be. I wasn't patient, and I still didn't trust God, the one I needed to trust the most. Even still, I never forgot the words God spoke to my heart through the Holy Spirit that night. He knew I would get tired and come to the end of Iva, and I did. He knew I would come to understand what I was truly thirsting for.

Not ready to surrender this area of my life, I turned my full focus to online dating. I thought I knew better than anyone, including God about men and relationships. I carried an arrogance in this area for years, believing that my past involvements made me an expert in this area. This pride made me stubborn and delayed my healing, afraid to pursue life without a man also kept me seeking companionship at any cost even if it meant using my body to keep a man close. I cannot sugar coat this area of sin because many are caught up in wanting a companion more then they want God. Anyone or anything that you worship or place on a pedestal in the altar of your heart becomes a sin of idolatry.

My first online dating encounter was with a great man of God from another state. We knew from the beginning it would never be a love connection between us, but he became such a source of strength for me as we struggled through our baggage and sexual issues where relationships were concerned. He also had been sexually abused at a young age.

I will never forget the time when I met another person online, and ended up becoming intimate with him and I shared this with the first guy that I mentioned above. His reaction startled me to wake up. He asked if I had used any type of protection when I engaged in this sexual encounter? I said, 'no' as if that was no big deal. He began to yell at me literally in the phone, "what is wrong with you? Why do you have a death wish upon your life? You could contract HIV or something else and there are those of us out here that actually care about you, so stop treating your life as if it is nothing."

I began to weep profusely because no man had ever stepped up in this area of my life and cared about what happened to me. He let me know I was valuable to God, to him and others and this reckless behavior had to end. The desire for something more began in that moment in time. I remained online for about three years before I shut it all down. Nothing was working out and I had become tired of trying to decipher the fake from the real profiles the men posted online. I grew tired of all the superficial attention, and the constant phone calls all times of the day and night.

Online dating is beneficial for some, as I witnessed two marriages of born-again believers coming out of it. With that being said though, a lot of the time it just seems to be a group of wounded souls, such as myself, feeding on other wounded souls and wandering into each other's lives. We truly needed to allow the true transforming work of the Holy Spirit to deliver and set us free once and for all.

The season of online dating concluded with me finally facing my fear of being alone. I quieted myself, changed my phone number, and email. Then I spent the time seeking what I really wanted to happen in my life going forward. I wanted to know stability, security and love. I wanted to know what God wanted for me; I wanted to know that I was worth being loved. My only barometer of worth had been my past involvement with men and their reaction to me. I wondered if God truly cared about how I felt? I lived so buried for years under layers of shame about what my life had amounted to. I knew that I could not erase what happened to me as a 14-year-old girl, but I was finally ready to heal and grow.

One day while rushing to get ready for a women's brunch where my former co-pastor was scheduled to speak, I began to struggle with my identity as a Christian woman again. This was a continual inward battleground for me whenever I was in the presence of other Christian women. Some of the battle was because of my awareness of my past. Other reasons I struggled was because of some of the things spoken to me by other Christian women who knew my past by what I had shared.

It was clear that I did not measure up to the religious standards of others as a woman of God. I thought I couldn't be used by God because of my yucky past and many divorces, so instead of embracing the scripture that speaks of God not having partiality of one over another (read **Acts 10:34**), I believed I was tainted and unqualified to receive the blessings of God in my life. Not wanting to stand out from the other women, I tried to mimic what I didn't comprehend at the time that I could authentically have.

The Samaritan Woman had an encounter with Jesus Christ Himself at Jacob's Well *(Read **John 4:1-19; 23-42**)*. The first thing that stood out for me about her was that her birth name wasn't mentioned in this passage of scripture. Our names mean everything to us. It is how we are identified along with our social security number, and yet her name was never mentioned. Instead, her identity came from her cultural background as a Samaritan, and she had been through quite a few husbands.

It was known that the Samaritans and the Jews had significant conflict with one another, yet that did not hold Jesus back from a divine encounter on that day at Jacob's Well. Like her, my identity had become connected to where I had come from and the things I had done in my past.

Let's look closer at this moment of awareness and restoration in her life through these passages of scriptures that became life to me.

> *John 4:1-4 Now when the Lord knew (learned, became aware) that the Pharisees had been told that Jesus was winning and baptizing more disciples than John—[2] Though Jesus Himself did not baptize, but His disciples—[3] He left Judea and returned to Galilee. [4] It was necessary for Him to go through Samaria (AMP).*

The shortest route from Judea in the south to Galilee in the north went through Samaria. Christ needed to go through Samaria if he wanted to travel the direct route. The Jews often avoided Samaria by going around along the Jordan River due to the hatred between the Jews and Samaritans, which went back to the time "of" exile.[2]

> *John 4:5-7 And in doing so, He arrived at a Samaritan town called Sychar, near the tract of land that Jacob gave to his son Joseph. [6] And Jacob's well was there. So, Jesus, tired as He was from His journey, sat down [to rest] by the well. It was then about the sixth hour (about noon). [7] Presently, when a woman of Samaria came along to draw water, Jesus said to her, "Give me a drink" (AMP).*

There was a divine and natural purpose in his stop that noonday. No one person is more important than another when it comes to Jesus and the gift of salvation. He has the supernatural ability to meet you where you are. Her cultural

---

[2] *The NKJV Study Bible*, Copyright @ 1997, 2007 by Thomas Nelson, Inc. Used by permission. All Rights Reserved. Notes on John 4:4, pg. 1663.

background, her current lifestyle, (she was living with a man) did not deter Jesus from having an encounter with the Samaritan woman on that day. He came for this specific woman, on this particular day, with a divine purpose. She was worth it.

> **John 4:8-10** *For His disciples had gone off into the town to buy food—[9] The Samaritan woman said to Him, "How is it that You, being a Jew, ask me, a Samaritan [and a] woman, for a drink?—For the Jews have nothing to do with the Samaritans—[10] Jesus answered her, "if you had only known and had recognized God's gift and who this is that is saying to you, Give Me a drink, you would have asked Him [instead] and He would have given you living water"* (AMP).

Jesus recognized her true thirst, and the natural water was not what she truly yearned for that day on her trip to Jacob's well (*see John 4:14*).

> **John 4:11-12** *She said to Him, "Sir, You have nothing to draw with [no drawing bucket] and the well is deep; how then can You provide living water? [Where do You get Your living water?] [12] Are You greater than and superior to our ancestor Jacob, who gave us this well and who used to drink from it himself, and his sons and his cattle also?"* **(AMP)**

She noticed that the man talking to her about something beyond her natural need, had nothing with Him to draw water from the well. How would He present this water that He offered her?

John 4:13-15 Jesus answered her, "All who drink of this water will be thirsty again.[14] But whoever takes a drink of the water that I will give him shall never, no never, be thirsty any more. But the water that I will give him shall become a spring of water welling up (flowing, bubbling) [continually] within him unto (into, for) eternal life." [15] The woman said to Him, "Sir, give me this water, so that I may never get thirsty nor have to come [continually all the way] here to draw" (AMP).

At this point of the encounter, the woman was still missing the message concerning the water that she truly needed. As long as our perceived needs are only seen through the natural realm, we miss the supernatural encounters and manifestations of God. Our needs are more in-depth than the natural fixes of life, as many of us have come to learn over time. She was still missing the message concerning the water that she truly needed at this point in the encounter.

Reflecting on my own life, Christ knew I was thirsty for something different when He drew me to the sustaining, eternal waters of life. I needed something besides the companionship of a man. I kept looking to fill my inner void with a new companion, which most times left me feeling more depleted and dehydrated than the last. What do you use to quench the thirst in your life?

John 4:16 At this, Jesus said to her, "Go, call your husband and come back here" (AMP).

Jesus mentioned the woman's many husbands and current living state to expose her weaknesses and His awareness of who she was.

> **John 4:17-19** *The woman answered, I have no husband. Jesus said to her, You have spoken truly in saying, I have no husband.[18] For you have had five husbands, and the man you are now living with is not your husband. In this you have spoken truly.[19] The woman said to Him, Sir, I see and understand that You are a prophet (AMP).*

Due to her life's condition being exposed, the woman surmised that Jesus was a prophet, a person divinely inspired with supernatural knowledge (*1 Sam. 9:9*).

> **John 4:25-30** *The woman said to Him, I know that Messiah is coming, He Who is called the Christ (the Anointed One); and when He arrives, He will tell us everything we need to know and make it clear to us.[26] Jesus said to her, I Who now speak with you am He.[27] Just then His disciples came and they wondered (were surprised, astonished) to find Him talking with a woman [a married woman]. However, not one of them asked Him, What are You inquiring about? What do You want? or, Why do You speak with her?[28] Then the woman left her water jar and went away to the town. And she began telling the people,[29] Come, see a Man Who has told me everything that I ever did! Can this be [is not this] the Christ? [Must not this be the Messiah, the Anointed One?][30] So the people left the town and set out to go to Him (AMP).*

On a regular day, the Samaritan woman at Jacob's Well experienced a life-giving encounter. Once Jesus entered the picture, she was transformed because she recognized the divine meeting. The One they were anticipating had arrived, and she had a personal moment with him. The Word of the Lord says she went back to the men in her town and told them of her encounter (*verse 28 KJV*). How defining was that? She was able to go back to the environment of her weakness and failures; where people only remembered who she used to be and what she used to do. They were able to witness the hand of God upon her life.

One Sunday when I was still a babe in Christ, a sister from church asked me to go with her to make a run to a grocery store. We had to pick up a couple of items for the gathering we were having at the church.

As soon as we hit the grocery store, I saw a former neighbor who lived in the same neighborhood where Joe and I had lived. He was an older gentleman that had lived a couple of doors away from our house. I said, "hello," not remembering his name, but recognizing him by his face. The sister with me knew him as well. The first thing out of his mouth to her was, "I remember her growing up in the neighborhood, and she was so fast, just boy crazy and a hot little something". I looked at the sister shocked and so embarrassed. I was trying to explain that I was a born-again Christian, but he just wanted to dwell on my past. I left devastated by this exposure.

Today, I know without a shadow of a doubt that my witness is sealed by the shed blood of Jesus Christ. Even though I have encountered others from my past who wanted to ignore my present victory and focus only on my past shame, I have learned to shake it off. I keep moving forward declaring that Jesus is Lord. I had to make peace with my past to be able to write this book. Jesus Christ entered my life and restored my identity in Him as a woman of faith, purpose and with destiny.

The Samaritan woman's change was impacting because the townspeople went looking for the Savior as a result of her testimony. Her identity was restored, and she became an influence amongst her people.

As you read this chapter, I hope you embrace the truth that no matter where you come from and what you have done in your past, Jesus Christ came that you may have life and have it more abundantly.

> *John 10: 9 – 11 I am the Door; anyone who enters through Me will be saved (will live). He will come in and he will go out [freely], and find pasture. [10] The thief comes only in order to steal and kill and destroy. I came that they may have and enjoy life, and have it in abundance (to the full, till it overflows). [11] I am The Good Shepherd. The Good Shepherd risks and lays down His [own] life for the sheep. (AMP)*

YOU have a new identity waiting in Him if you will take the first step and receive Him as Lord over your life.

Chapter Three

The Leah Syndrome
That Rejection Thing

Another day was already upon her before she could catch her breath from yesterday. Slowly rolling the comforter from around her face, she stretched to ease the unbearable tension that yet remained in her body. This tension represented the same type of tension in their house. Once again, she found herself alone in their bed at the break of dawn. The pillow next to her didn't even show an indentation from the usual occupant. "It must have been *her* night," she sadly spoke to no one.

She swung her legs out from under the covers and planted her feet on the floor. They danced around for a bit as they sought the warm, plush shelter of her favorite, blue house shoes. They had been a gift from him. What she didn't realize when he presented them to her, was that those house shoes would be more of a companion to her than he ever had any intentions of being to her. They came gift-wrapped, with a matching plush bathrobe that had her name *Maria* so delicately engraved across the top. The shoes brought comfort to her feet but not to her heart.

Maria shuffled to the bathroom with slow, deliberate steps and finally looked up to peer at her reflection in the mirror. She stood motionless for a long time. The dialogue between her and her reflection in the mirror started instantly: "So just what does she have that you don't?" She turned her head from side to side, analyzing each angle. "Mirror, we are not having this conversation today, while you look me up and down and judge me for the widening of my hips from having his babies, or the sagging of my milk-producing breasts that no longer carry the luster of my youth."

Slightly shifting again, she turned to her side, looked at her form and recognized the protruding pouch of her stomach. She took a deep breath and sucked her stomach in as hard as she could, but her stomach never acknowledged the effort, and just remained in its protruding state.

Maria knew she needed to stop this harsh self-examination, but she did it every time she knew he was with *her*. What is the thing about Celeste that causes this man to disrespect our children and me when he returned to us after each excursion with her? Not even trying to hide his moments of betrayals.

Facing forward, the tears she cried on many occasions began to gently flow from the ducts of her eyes, blinding her vision. The tears represented the betrayal she felt by Jake and came from the sea of hurt she was experiencing once again.

Sobbing uncontrollably now, *Maria* screamed out the names of each of her three babies: Junior, Michael, and Ava. She had given him these children when he asked and even demanded it of her. Baby after baby found its way into the world and yet he still loved *her*. Celeste was her name.

Jake had loved Celeste since childhood. They all grew up together in the old neighborhood, on the north side of the city, back in the day. He said it all started when they were in the fifth grade on the playground. During a kickball game she slid into his base and his heart sealed itself around hers. She was the one with the long pigtails and caramel colored skin that glistened. They became inseparable.

It was right after high school that Jake was challenged. Celeste answered the call of education abroad, and left him in the U.S. to work his job at the insurance firm. He begged and pleaded for Celeste to wait to go overseas; his heart felt faint at the thought of a life separated from her. He was genuinely in love with Celeste and could not imagine life without her close.

On the other hand, Celeste felt the push of the wind propelling her to soar to the highest heights, and she could not wait to become all she was called to be. Picking up the shattered pieces of his broken heart and unspoken dreams of a life with Celeste, Jake set an inner vow; he would never love like that ever again and he would protect his heart at all costs.

Then *Maria* reconnected back into his life. Having experienced repeated offenses of rejection throughout much of her life, she was desperate for the love of a man. Yes, she hated to admit it but any man would do, if she could pretend to know love for a brief second in her day. Jake was different, so she threw all caution to the wind. It was as if Maria forgot the rejection she felt time and time again in her former relationships with men where she felt rejected. With Jake, she was determined to win his heart away from Celeste.

Now this could be anyone's story, as I was thinking about the story of Leah, Jacob and Rachel in the Bible in the book of Genesis 29:1-30. This would be a great moment to grab your Bible and follow along. I feel like I can relate to Maria or Leah, and if we all met today at a café over some warm mocha latte, we would have a lot to talk about when it comes to feelings of rejection in relationships.

The story of Maria, Jake and Celeste is also very reflective of how timeless the Bible is when we find ourselves struggling with similar life situations. Many women can relate to Maria or Leah as the rejected ones in these two distinct stories, but I also want you to understand that our Heavenly Father also recognizes and cares when we feel rejection.'

For many years, the spirit of rejection had me striving to get men who were not into me at all to love me. I learned valuable lessons during these times of feeling stuck in situations very much like Leah's. The men were not at fault for my unhappiness when they were upfront with me from the beginning. So, what have I learned?

Years ago, while getting to know someone, one day the Holy Spirit said to me, "Iva do not listen to what he says, listen to what he does." Pay attention to his actions toward you and not just the things that he speaks out of his mouth. You will know where you stand when you observe what is demonstrated. When a man tells you he is not interested in getting to know you better, he wants to "kick it with you" (meaning have sex only), or says that he "just wants to be friends"; we as women must learn to believe what he says whether it is what we hoped for or not. Men know what they do or do not want in a relationship with someone. They are not challenging us to prove them wrong by throwing ourselves at them anyway.

There was a great book that helped me even more with these realizations entitled, "He's Just Not That Into You" by Greg Behrendt and Liz Tuccillon. While reading, I began recognizing some of the signs the authors presented. I'd seen these telltale signs of men's actions toward me and it was another A-HA moment of reality for me.

Learning to accept the truth of a man's desires toward you will help prevent you from wasting time, energy and resources that should be reserved for the right man. If a man wants you, he will choose you and come after you with all that is within him. I knew I deserved love, but at the same time, I didn't quite believe it would happen to me.

I was at work one morning when I was silently crying while working on the assembly line. I was struggling because I met a man in another state through an online dating website. I quickly let my guard down and connected emotionally, which was a pattern for me when dealing with men. Becoming emotionally invested right away instead of guarding my heart, as we are admonished in *Proverbs 4:23, "Keep your heart with all diligence, For out of it spring the issues of life,"* invites rejection out of a neediness to be validated by the acceptance of a man.

About a month into this relationship, I began to sense something was not right, but I really enjoyed someone giving me attention. He was disappearing and we were having inconsistent dialogue. The inconsistency would pull me close in the realm of hope and then I felt rejected through the reality of his actions. One day after all of the back and forth, he said, "You're not the one." Now being transparent, I must admit I never met this man in person and yet I sent him money and a couple of gifts trying to win him over. That's how desperate I was.

It was an emotionally unstable time for me meeting so many different men online. Being performance-driven and having my identity wrapped up in people's approval, I became 'the everything girl' especially with men. Because I feared rejection, I presented myself to be the type of woman he wanted even when I knew that was not true to my core.

For example, if he liked outdoors, I would pretend to love the outdoors to win him over, not realizing the truth would expose my fake identity. His remarks that I would never be his wife after the things I had done for him had me feeling very rejected and foolish. While crying before God I asked, "Why does this keep happening to me?" I heard the words, "It's the Leah Syndrome", and the Lord even took me back into the archives of my memories to the root of its start in my life:

I had been involved with someone in the past who told me he was going to marry me while he secretly had promised himself to someone else and placed a ring on her finger and set a wedding date. When I found out I was gravely wounded inwardly and developed what I call 'yucky dialogue' that I was not good enough because of my past. I was good enough for him to lay with, but not good enough to be his wife.

So just what is "The Leah Syndrome?" According to Webster's New World Dictionary and Thesaurus, a syndrome is defined as a set of symptoms characterizing a disease or condition. *The Leah Syndrome* is something I use to describe a set of thoughts, behaviors and ideas rooted in rejection, that lead to a destructive need to accept real or fake love at any cost. It tends to culminate in rejection and requires working through those issues.

Leah experienced rejection by her husband Jacob who was in love with her sister. No matter what Leah did, she fought to get him to love her and it consumed her life's decisions and choices. Each of her children represented the pain of trying to win this man's love.

We must find positive and productive ways to work through rejection without crumbling under its weight. Oftentimes, the sufferer cannot fight their way out of this cycle as they continue to enter relationship after relationship until they are ready to face their fear of loneliness, while working through heartaches, and low self-esteem in a healthy, productive manner.

In **Genesis 29**, we learn about Leah's story. She is the older sister of Rachel, and both women end up as wives to Jacob. Jacob falls in love with Rachel first and agrees to wait and work seven years to marry her. (Now, who wouldn't want a man to fight for her like that?) Laban, the father of the two women, devises a plan; in their custom, the older daughter was to be married before the younger daughter (Genesis 29:26).

When the seven years is up, Laban deceives Jacob by giving him Leah instead of Rachel. The two consummate their marriage by deception before Jacob realizes what has happened. He's angry, but Laban is ready for him, he tells Jacob that he can still have Rachel but must work another seven years (*Genesis 27-28*).

Jacob's love for Rachel is so deep that he agrees to this deal. He loved Rachel, but he accepted Leah out of obligation. God saw the love Leah desired and was aware of how Leah felt so He blessed her by opening her womb. At that time, having the ability to bear children was the most blessed thing for a woman to be able to do. If one were barren, she would be considered cursed.

> *Genesis 29:31-35," And when the Lord saw that Leah was despised, He made her able to bear children, but Rachel was barren".* And Leah became pregnant and bore a son and named him Reuben; for she said, Because the Lord has seen my humiliation and affliction; now my husband will love me. *[Leah] became pregnant again and bore a son and said, Because the Lord heard that I am despised, He has given me this son also; and she named him Simeon [God hears]. And she became pregnant again and bore a son and said, now this time will my husband be a companion to me, for I have borne him three sons. Therefore, he was named Levi [companion]. Again, she conceived and bore a son, and she said, now will I praise the Lord! So, she called his name Judah [praise]; then [for a time] she ceased bearing. (AMP)*

These were just the first four children that Leah was glad to bear to win the heart of her husband, a heart that was given so willingly to her sister Rachel, but not to her. All of this stirred competition between she and Rachel. Rachel was barren during the beginning of the marriage, but eventually God heard her prayers as well and she had two sons by Jacob.

Leah felt rejected and who can blame her? Her rejection made her question her self-worth. She thought that bearing children would make Jacob love her, but she should have seen what a blessing her children were all on their own. Rejection and all its symptoms cause us to make decisions about who we think we are instead of who God says we are.

The Spirit of Rejection is a deadly killer that takes the very beauty and essence of life, and chokes it until no real life remains. In Leah's case, the rejection did not begin with Jacob, but it began with her own flesh and blood, her father.

Women today are always being compared to one another, and it places us in a perpetual state of rejection. There is always something or someone telling us what's wrong with us and why the next woman is so much better. The 'problems' we're told we have can range from our appearance, beliefs, or even our ambitions. We're placed on pedestals and then knocked to the ground.

We live in a culture that places great emphasis on women; but many times that comes from the physical appearance before our intellect, character, integrity or spirituality is factored in. If we are not aware, the spirit of rejection can cause us to use the standards of the world as a measure for our own value and self-worth. Instead, we must learn to use the Word of God as a standard concerning our value and worth.

I did not handle rejection well for a very long time. The last man I was married to was very emotionally and verbally abusive. His lips would tell me he loved me all the time, but his actions told the real story. When our marriage was finally over, my head was hung down so low; I had gone through eight years of rejection. Although I was his wife, I felt no respect or honor for my position in his life.

Sometime after our final separation, something strange started to happen. I was out in public and riding an escalator when a stranger shouted to me and said, "You are so beautiful." I looked at him and gave him the crazy eye while wondering, 'Where did that come from?' A few days later while standing in line, I was approached by another stranger who said, "Wow, you are so beautiful" and then walked away.

Once again I was baffled. Finally, after a few more instances of this I realized it was God reaching from Heaven with His hand of love. He was lifting my hung down head with what I called, 'Love Pats from my Father.' God cares about the rejection you have felt in your life no matter the source, and He does not want that to be your final dialogue. There is a fulfilling life after rejection, and I am a living witness.

It took my renewed commitment to God and myself to recognize that rejection was not my final dialogue, so it could no longer define me. I had the love of God on my side, and that made me priceless. God loved me without reservation whether I deserved it or not. He had a plan for me that I had deviated from because I sought earthly love over divine love, and when I turned back to Him, He taught me how to receive His love and how to love myself.

This was not an overnight revelation for me, and some days I'm still challenged in this area. It has taken me years of effort (with some failure) along with biblical counseling, a loving family, and praying friends to help me overcome the years of pain from being rejected by men. Once some of the other problems connected to denial were also identified and renounced, I received tools to help me walk out the moments when rejection would rear its head.

I must also add that sometimes rejection is good for growth and protection against some entanglements that God wants to keep us from. We can find ourselves in these compromising positions due to our lack of discernment. The great part in all of this is that He can turn it for our good if we let Him (*Romans 8:28*).

The man I met online had a story that I was unaware of, and his rejection left me crying and pining over losing him. I didn't realize it then, but it turned out to be a blessing. About a year or so after we stopped communicating, he reached out to talk. He wanted me to know he had found a special lady and gotten married. His purpose for contacting me was the play that we worked on when we were communicating in the past. He told his wife about the play and me, and wanted to see if we could complete the play and turn it into a gospel production for young people. I agreed to help.

One day, after a couple of months passed since we'd last spoken, I heard a 'ding' from my laptop. I recognized that sound as the alert from an instant message. To my surprise, I saw his email address pop up and thought, 'Okay, there he is' when the Holy Spirit revealed, "No, that's his wife".

I responded to the IM, and she shared her name and that she was his widow. She told me that he had died a couple months ago. I was speechless. Then through further dialogue, I found out she was not his third wife as he shared when we first met. He had been deceptive with both her and me. She discovered, after his death, that she was actually his sixth wife, and he had never divorced wife number five. We agreed to speak the next day by phone and exchanged phone numbers.

When we spoke, our conversation was over four hours long as we cried, shared and ministered to one another. I had dreams about this man along the way that let me know something was not quite right about him. I knew God was warning me to be careful. The blessing has been this unusual friendship that has evolved between she and I over the years. She is one of my most beautiful and sincere sisters in Christ with a tremendous calling on her life. Only God could turn my rejection from this man into a story of beauty and healing for his former wife and me.

Watch this as I share a blessing that came through this time of Leah's rejection from her husband.

> **Genesis 29:35**, *Again she conceived and bore a son, and she said, now will I praise the Lord! So she called his name Judah [praise]; then [for a time] she ceased bearing. (AMP)*

Jesus Christ came through the lineage of Leah's son Judah (*see Matthew 1:1-3.*) What an honor it must be to know the Lord and Savior, who came to redeem the entire world, came here through the lineage of her baby. God is always faithful when we include him in everything that we face. All the sons of Leah, Rachel, and their maidens represent the 12 tribes of Israel. Through rejection came destiny and purpose despite Leah's pain.

The following journal entry was written while I was still struggling concerning the online man. God spoke to my heart with His promises that would come to pass in my life nine years later.

I have learned how to embrace the unconditional love of Christ in my life, and I have learned that people are not responsible for how I feel about myself. I am responsible for the dialogue I speak to myself each day. The Spirit of Rejection will always be there to challenge us in this life, but we must remember there is life long after the moments of discomfort. May you take this journal entry and grasp these promises from

God as your own. Hear Him speaking to your heart and let your healing process begin.

April 13, 2007, Tuesday - Listening time God's love for me!

My love for you surpasses the depths and heights of anything you've ever known or have hoped to know. It surpasses every disappointment and failure experienced because of a man. It is glued to you in its entirety, set to heal, deliver, set free and return you unto me. You will adorn my love in your retiring time and in your uprising.

You don't have to wait upon another man to validate what I have already claimed and received as mines for you Iva. You do belong to me now and forever more. Let them go, do not hold onto them. Those that must go, MUST go, but only those that I have approved can stay.

I hear and have heard your cries night after night longing for the one who will love you completely... I AM HE!

You are about to give birth, and no earthly man has planted the seed in your womb, it is a glorious divine seed created from Heaven.

You asked why you?

Because I have had an everlasting love for you since the beginning of time. I placed it all within you even before you were ever created. It will leave a lasting impact on many and change the course of their lives. You cannot see this work through the natural eye but only through the eyes of the spirit can it be seen. At times, it shall be intense and never ending but my grace is sufficient for you to see your task through.

Men will come and men will go but my constant love shall remain forever. Listen, I care about everything that affects you no matter how little or simple it may appear to be. Every tear you drop and every moan you sigh out of your mouth I care about, because my love for you is intense. You will grow in leaps and bounds in the days ahead, and you will notice this growth and its impact on others. Satan will send false prophets and hopefuls your way to try and deter your path, but NOT so, his schemes will not succeed but they will merely fall by the wayside.

There will be up days and down days, but my glory SHALL be revealed through your life. Peace be still, joy shall remain. Allow my words to abide now in you and yes you may ask what you will and it shall be given according to my plans for you.

I know you question if I am speaking this long to you, but there is much to say in a short time and I have been waiting for you to listen.

Please remember that no weapon formed against you will prosper (*read Isaiah 54:17*) I know that the future seems uncertain right in this moment in time but it shall be revealed in due time. Your latter shall be greater.

ALL THINGS WORK TOGETHER FOR THE GOOD OF THEM WHO LOVE GOD AND ARE CALLED ACCORDING TO MY PURPOSES.

Chapter Four

The Choice Factor
Choosing to Change

Slowly, I pulled my car up to Joe's house years after we had parted ways. Our physical contact had ceased, but the soul-tie to this man ran very deep. He was standing outside chatting with a couple of his buddies doing what he loved to do best, sipping on a beer with one hand and balancing a cigarette in the other.

The men with him were looking at me, but one knew exactly who I was. It had been some time, and I was no longer the 14-year old child, but an adult in her early 30's. I cannot recall how I felt at that moment in time facing this man, but I'm sure it wasn't an easy decision for me to meet my past head-on. Something propelled me to want to confront Joe that day.

His friends treated me as if I was their age and had been in a regular adult relationship with this man. How did they miss the 20-year difference in our age? I got out of the car and approached the group. I made small talk while his friends were present and then they gave Joe and me our space. I was angry because my life was so jacked up, and I wanted Joe to take some responsibility for turning me out at such a young age without any consideration for the consequences in my life. He had a daughter. Would he have wanted that for her?

I have always been outspoken when I needed to be, and that day I was the same, and he listened. I remember it was summer time and we stood outside of the house where everything had taken place some years before. I believe Joe apologized, but I can't recall the depth of sincerity.

Sometime later, I woke up one morning with Joe on my mind but in a different capacity. I was precise about my attire that day. My make-up flawless, my clothing picked with care. I was dressed to impress with a large straw hat on my head, the front left low enough to hide my shame behind one eye, yet looking like I had just stepped off the runway. I was in shock and numb.

I drove that morning to the historic brick church sitting on the corner and found a place to park amidst all the cars already there and got out. I strolled up the stairs of that grand entrance as if I was a celebrity of some sort there to disturb the atmosphere. Once inside, I slowly walked to the front of the church and stared down at the casket before me, and there he lay in a suit. Joe was dead!

This was around 17 years after Joe had done his sexual work on me. I stood over Joe's casket looking down at him while inwardly cussing up a storm. At that moment in time no one else even existed in that space, it was just he and I. Lashing out at the destruction he brought into my life; I felt he had gotten what he deserved for what he did to me and never paid the price for. I was pissed.

He was able to start a life with someone else, and I was nursing two failed marriages by then. I completed my inward rant and was sure he was on the way to hell for eternal damnation. I was not a born-again believer at that time. I turned and walked across the room and sat down on a pew trying to hold my composure and dignity in place as a spectator to this man's funeral. I was still in shock that this was my closure, or was it?

I began to wonder about the hidden safe that Joe kept in his house. On the inside of that safe were naked pictures of me taken when I was 14. Joe could have gone to prison. He knew this because he kept them under lock and key. Death was his best bet. I wondered if his young wife ever found the pictures of me, and if she knew who I was in that church that day. I can only hope the pictures were destroyed.

Joe had one friend who I would see out over the years after his death. We would always greet one another, and he would smile at me as if we had some form of a connection because of

Joe. He would ask how I was doing? I would give some necessary response, and then he would end our brief encounter with the strangest statement, "those sure were some good ole days".

The first time he said that to me, I walked away dumbfounded thinking good ole days for who? A couple more years passed, and when I ran into that friend again he gave me that same quirky line. I never responded to his statement to me, I let him believe what he wanted until the last time I saw him. By then I was a born-again believer.

Rushing into a restaurant to grab lunch before work one day, I saw him there with his wife. He approached me at the buffet counter with the same type of exchange as all our other encounters, but something inside of me snapped that day. I was in a confrontational mode, and I asked him did he even know how old I was when I was with Joe? I told him, as my words reflected the hurt and anger I still harbored deep within, that my life had been a mess because of Joe.

Suddenly, it was as if lightning had just struck him. I believe I saw tears well up in his eyes and he said he was so sorry. He asked how I was doing now and I told him I was a born-again believer, where I worked, and that I was surviving as I raised my two daughters. I didn't expect to see the water in his eyes. He then told me he was ill, and I was sorry to hear that. He then said, "Sometimes men see things from a different viewpoint, and I am so sorry again and glad to know you are doing better".

I watched him walk back to the table where his wife sat, and I wondered if he would share with her why his eyes were full of tears. I walked out the door glad that I finally spoke up for myself. How could those men who hung out with Joe not see that something about this was inappropriate? My tone that day in the restaurant was full of anger and venom, and I realized I wasn't over this as much as I thought I was. I had forgiven Joe somewhat, but it never even occurred to me that I needed to forgive his friends who knew the sin and kept the secret. I needed to forgive the fact that they never thought I was worth being protected as a child.

The Choice Factor chapter was birthed from the realization that even though one may have experienced life-altering events at the hands of others, one must examine the power they choose to give to victimizers. Harboring unforgiveness produces bitterness and unhappiness in the victim, not necessarily in the one who caused the harm. Sometimes these emotions can even trigger physical symptoms in the natural body. It is important to choose to change any unproductive mindsets toward those who have caused you harm.

I was a victim as a little girl, touched inappropriately by the hands of a hospital priest. I was a victim at the hands of some others, and then I was a victim at the hands of the neighbor. I saw victimization as a huge giant with broad shoulders. The shoulders represented a place of enormous power and strength, and I found a resting place for years as a victim on the shoulders of victimization.

My viewpoint in life for years had been nothing more than being a victim. The challenge for me, 20 or 30 years later, was to examine *how I could still stand on the shoulders of this giant called victimization and justify the power I was feeding it every day to remaining a victim.* I wanted to be victorious, but I could not claim being a victim and being victorious at the same time. The two cannot co-exist in harmony. You are either one or the other and you must decide which one you choose to be. God created us with the ability to make choices, and so our lives are a culmination of our choices and the results therein.

> *Deuteronomy 30:15, [**Choose Life**] "Listen closely, I have set before you today life and prosperity (good), and death and adversity (evil) (AMP).*

My heart weighed heavy for years with all the failures in my relationships. With each one of them, I brought my unresolved baggage neatly packed in full force. In my mind, it was the job of my partners to unpack my stuff and take it in stride, while I created a no tolerance zone for their baggage. They couldn't even bring theirs in the room.

Another way to see it was they were going to pay the price for what the previous partners had done. A room full of my baggage and the baggage of new love left no room for the adventure and growth of a new relationship in a healthy environment. After awhile, the new relationship suffocates and dies because of the lack of oxygen and lack of freedom to be the individuals we were called to be in our relationship. I needed to make some different choices, choices that demanded my attention and hard, committed work with the guidance of the Holy Spirit, if I wanted to see some different results.

Many have heard the definition of insanity is when you do the same thing over and over expecting a different result. It was unreasonable and selfish of me to think I could continue to enter relationships the same way as always and get a different result without unpacking my baggage so that I could breathe in a relationship without the weights of my past. Where would I even start with these significant pieces of baggage I carried into each of my former, failed marriages and all new relationships in between?

I was a born-again believer now, and God was welcomed into my life for my complete deliverance and healing. I sought out God's guidance, the Word of God, the Holy Spirit, and biblical counseling; something I had not done before. My pastors at the time had taken me as far as I could go; I needed a specialist who could go more in-depth toward those roots wrapped around my heart, choking the very life out of me. A part of the counseling process was to identify my baggage.

Let's walk through my baggage area and see some of the issues I needed to address first. Your list may be different, but unpack we must!

ANGER

Anger can be one of the most volatile human emotions that carry such a weight of responsibility with it. Things can be spoken, and actions displayed in anger that can have life-destroying effects to the receiver and giver of that anger. There is righteous anger when we see injustices in the world, but that was not the type of anger I was harboring.

My anger swelled up through the years after the first act of molestation against me by the priest in my hospital bed. I was angry for being the target of all these different men who were supposed to cover and protect me as a child and instead took advantage of me. I felt marked most of my life, and I was upset about it.

It's hard to admit this next one, but I was also angry at God for letting each one of them get away with touching me, and for the effects that lingered in my life into my early 50's. I was angry that I responded in the natural and developed sexual appetites through those experiences. I was mad at the people whom I should have been able to trust concerning my children after I found out they had violated them. As unfair as it all was, and as justified as I felt nursing my anger, the Bible challenged me to choose to change.

> *Colossians 3:8,* *But now you must put them all away: anger, wrath, malice, slander, and obscene talk from your mouth (AMP).*

Ephesians 4:31-32, Let all bitterness and wrath and anger and clamor and slander be put away from you, along with all malice. Be kind to one another, tenderhearted, forgiving one another, as God in Christ forgave you (AMP).

Ephesians 4:26-27, When angry, do not sin; do not ever let your wrath (your exasperation, your fury or indignation) last until the sun goes down. 27, Leave no [such] room or foothold for the devil [give no opportunity to him] (AMP).

We are admonished in the Word of God to put anger away, which means we must choose to change that area in our life and put action behind that choice. Regardless of the reason for that anger, I decided to release the poison of anger. The peace and joy of the Lord can grow and thrive within you when you release anger. Also, because anger can be connected to unforgiveness, this is the next piece of baggage I had to confront within me.

UNFORGIVENESS

This one here is a biggie for so many people. How do you forgive those who have hurt or harmed you, whether intentional or unintentional? Forgiving is a choice, but it is also a command. Most times we wrestle with the loss of what we feel was taken from us by another. We want what we lost back or for the thief to pay. The Holy Spirit never hesitates to bring back to my remembrance all the ways I have been forgiven when I want to drag my feet concerning the forgiveness of others.

I learned the Lord's Prayer in **Matthew 6:9-13** as a small child. I recited it as I was taught out of obedience without any understanding of the words in the entire prayer. I was a child, so everything was from the mind of a child. The challenge comes in as an adult, and the childish mindsets must be put away. Now, I become accountable for what I have learned and come to understand in the Lord's Prayer.

> *Matthew 6:12, And forgive us our debts, as we also have forgiven (left, remitted, and let go of the debts, and have given up resentment against) our debtors (AMP).*

The *New King James Version* of this same passage says, *"And forgive us our debts, as we forgive our debtors."*

It's made very clear: You must forgive those who have harmed you if you desire the Father in Heaven to forgive you for the things you have done to harm others. I know we love to see ourselves in a good light while peering through a magnifying glass to expose the faults of others. It's an all or nothing choice. Forgive and be forgiven… or chose not to forgive and not be forgiven. I decided to forgive, and in the heart of my struggle, I asked Jesus for help.

SHAME

I wore shame like a cloak, trying to hide behind the layers of its covering. Spending years working to appear perfect to guard my secrets any way I could. I didn't want too many people to know where I came from because I thought the judgments would come. In my mind, you could experience failures and indiscretions in life, but they could not be sexual in nature, especially if you were a woman.

During my walk as a believer, God began to deal with me and my baggage of shame. He promised me that I would forget the shame of my youth, and that I would walk in double honor for my shame.

> *Isaiah 54:4*, *"Do not be afraid; you will not be put to shame. Do not fear disgrace; you will not be humiliated. You will forget the shame of your youth and remember no more the reproach of your widowhood"* (NIV).

> *Isaiah 61:7*, *Instead of your shame you will receive a double portion, and instead of your disgrace you will rejoice in your inheritance. And so you will inherit a double portion in your land, and everlasting joy will be yours* (NIV).

I will accept no more shame and condemnation for my past. That baggage is too heavy to lug around for a lifetime. This realization took more time to unpack because the roots of shame and the fear of being found out dictated a lot of the steps and twist and turns of my existence. God promised us double honor for our shame.

IDOLATRY

It was a brother in Christ who showed me why my need to always have a man in my life was a form of *idolatry*. I was afraid to be alone and didn't even want to try. The Bible has a lot to say about worshipping anyone or anything above God. I refused for a very long time to learn how to be alone, which would later become an anchor of peace for me.

To be single, saved and lonely was not a winning combination in my book. I rushed into marriages that failed because of it, and wasted time and resources in relationships to avoid being alone. I trusted in those men more then I believed the God that I said I loved.

Being single, saved and celibate today, has been one of the most gratifying choices of my life to date, but it came with a price tag of many tears, frustrations, spiritual warfare, and so much more. Learning to let God keep me, and trusting Him was the best decision in my adult life that broke many destructive cycles.

> *Deuteronomy 6:4-6, Hear, O Israel: the Lord our God is one Lord [the only Lord]. [5]And you shall love the Lord your God with all your [mind and] heart and with your entire being and with all your might. [6] And these words which I am commanding you this day shall be [first] in your [own] minds and hearts: [then] (AMP).*

> *Exodus 34:14, (for you shall worship no other god, for the Lord whose name is Jealous, is a jealous God) (NKJV).*

We belong to God, who is a jealous God. No man or woman should ever be more important than your need for Him.

FORNICATION

The counterpart to fornication is lust, the driving force behind it all. Sexual sins become an ungodly anchor to your soul and mind. Sleeping with a person who you are not married to creates an illegal covenant that is not easily broken. You are now tied to that sexual partner with a soul tie.

You must choose to end sexual involvement with anyone you are not married to. This is non-negotiable if you want to grow in your relationship with God. I have had people tell me: God knows I need to test drive or have at least one sexual encounter with my future mate. My response always is, find me the scripture in the Bible that says fornication is a sin except for

_____ (*enter your name in the blank*), and I will stand in agreement with you that God approves.

No one has yet been able to write their name on the dotted line and justify their sexual sins. This is another one of those massive pieces of baggage you must choose to unpack. The Word of God has much to say about lust and fornication.

> *1 Thessalonians 4:3-6, It is God's will that you should be sanctified: that you should avoid sexual immorality; that each of you should learn to control your own body in a way that is holy and honorable, not in passionate lust like the pagans, who do not know God; and that in this matter no one should wrong or take advantage of a brother or sister. The Lord will punish all those who commit such sins, as we told you and warned you before (NIV).*

God loves us and tries to protect us by sharing the truth of His word and what is required to honor it, which starts with a choice to obey or not. You are accountable for what you know. I had to repent before God, stop making excuses, bring my flesh under submission, and seek His strength to overcome. He has been faithful to keep me for years now, and will continue until the day I may or may not marry again.

I chose, and He honored that choice. It was not easy, and I missed the mark before I got it right, but today I am content that I am no longer using my body to indulge in the sins of my flesh. If I can do it, so can you.

> *1 Corinthians 6:19-20, Or do you not know that your body is a temple of the Holy Spirit who is in you, whom you have from God, and that you are not your own? For you have been bought with a price: therefore glorify God in your body (NASB).*

> *Galatians 5:16, I say then: Walk in the Spirit, and you shall not fulfill the lust of the flesh (NKJV).*

We have uncovered some of the baggage that I had to unpack and address, no longer being oblivious to its weightiness in my life. Freedom always comes at a price, and you have to decide for your life how free do you want to be and are you ready to pay the price?

Chapter Five

My $10,000.00 Breakthrough

From the Mind of Poverty to Prosperity

Strange title I know huh?

This breakthrough chapter is only partially about money. After years of a poverty mindset in every area of my life, spirit, soul and body; God used the broken places in my heart to show me how I have tried to cope instead of surrendering to Him. Who knew that this chapter in my life would become the catalyst that God would use to bring forth the breakthroughs that I would later walk out in my life.

From the time I was in high school, I wanted to have a house with a husband, 2.5 kids (never figured out what the .5 represented), a dog, and of course I must have the white picket fence. Most of us have been raised to believe it is the ultimate and only American dream, and if you by some chance miss attaining that you are abnormal in what is deemed to be an otherwise ordinary world.

I was in search of that normalcy to feel and appear ordinary, and owning a home was a part of that dream. If I could only accomplish that, I would finally validate my graduation to stability, which had eluded me my whole life, or so I thought. My problem, how could I achieve this with a poverty mentality in every area of my life.

To backtrack a little, from the time I came to the planet I had always lived in nice homes, we never knew poverty. We struggled sometimes, but never experienced poverty. When I came in the world, I remember the house my parents lived in had top-notch creature comforts. In 1958, both of my parents worked outside of the home and had good jobs.

After my parents split and divorced, we still lived in a nice duplex (a two-family dwelling structure). When my mother remarried, they bought a lovely home that was perfectly set in a multicultural neighborhood, and four years later this is where the violation with Joe occurred.

Later, we moved into an upscale historic, gated community with beautiful homes, roads made of brick, and my favorite spot, an isle in the middle of all the houses in our section with a couple of park benches. I loved going across the street to the isle to study my homework in the evenings, it was so peaceful for me. Though my natural surroundings were pleasant, my inner house was a mess.

Once on my own, while raising my daughters, I lived for many years with what I called a rental company mentality. This is when you rent-to-own items because of a lack of creditworthiness, and you make payments by the week (or bi-weekly) with colossal interest added by the time you have completed your purchase. A $300 television may end up costing you $800 before it is all over. With weekly or bi-weekly payments, you don't factor in the $500 in interest that you have to give in order to take that item home on loan.

It would be later in life before I would even begin to check my credit and find out what a good credit score was all about, as well as how to maintain good credit.

Rental items and a man were as far as my vision for my life went at that time. So many years and resources were thrown recklessly away on men that I tried to buy and keep. My life vision after becoming employed at General Motors was hard to change because of my poverty mindset. Taking care of my girls the best I could, and keeping a man close enough to feel wanted was my only focus. I didn't put money away, I lived paycheck to paycheck, unable to comprehend stewardship and ownership.

Years later, I began to dream of something more, I just wasn't sure where to start to obtain that something more. By my third marriage, I was trying to prove I was like other women that had it together. The first home I had built from the ground up was an experience rooted in delusion and emotional pain because of my broken marriage.

It was around 1995, and my husband and I were going through another separation. I saw a pamphlet on revitalization in the inner city by having homes built for over a $100,000 with tax breaks that would set me up in a place for actual homeownership. I wanted so much to feel normal in my 30's, so I started the process, which I was unprepared for mentally and financially, and it showed when I could not finish the process.

I began meeting with the neighborhood group spearheading the project, and then with the builder. I was purchasing a $114,000 home. I had a tenacious hope everything would just happen for me without money management skills, no down payment, and no emergency savings. I had only my ability to dream big and bite off more than I could chew.

While yet in the preparation stages, I shared the house idea with my estranged husband and we decided to reconcile, and he got in on this deal of my making. I never asked God if this was His will for me from the very beginning because I was chasing normalcy in my mind and soul apart from God. I merely wanted God to co-sign my plans. Have you ever been there?

Psalm 127:1a, "Unless the Lord builds the house, they labor in vain who build it" (NKJV).

When we invite Jesus Christ to be the head of our life, we must allow Him to do just that. One of my hardest lessons to learn is that **you can never medicate inner pain through outer props**. I still remember going to the house site one Sunday after church as a family, and we prayed in a circle over the ground and named it and claimed it for our new home. (We were in the "name it and claim it" era of the church at that time.)

We went to the builders and began to select the counters, the flooring, the master suite dimensions and so forth. We shared our ideas and color schemes on every detail of this house from the inside out; as if we were on one accord as a couple having an HGTV moment. My daughters and I drove by often watching and taking pictures as it was being built from the ground up. This home was to represent my wholeness (while yet not whole).

As the final touches were put into place on the house, my ex-husband made it clear that after careful consideration he had no desire to buy this house and live in it with us. I had to finally come to the realization that I could never afford to purchase this house on my own, and so we had to walk away from it. This caused me embarrassment from the attention in the media because I was one of three who were kicking off this revitalization program, and it had been covered through various media outlets.

Of the three houses built right next to each other on the

block, I had to watch my future neighbors move into their newly built homes as another family moved into the home I was supposed to occupy. That stung worst then a million bee stings.

As I walked away from the custom built home that was now for someone else's enjoyment, I imprisoned my heartbreak from this significant disappointment, and built more jail bars to keep my heart enclosed. This also included from God, and then I moved on, numb. A few years later, after still being in and out with husband number three, we finally divorced and I started the process again of trying to obtain a home (my fix for normalcy).

Once again, I had the opportunity to be a part of customizing a villa that had already been built from the ground up. The outer structure was already in place; I just needed to customize the inside. In every place I invested, I was always thinking of some man stepping into my preconceived fantasy and taking his place in my world at the head of MY home. See how crazy that sounds? Yet, that is how I saw life back then.

I moved into my new villa with the understanding that I would purchase it in one year. It was a lease to own deal, and yes I was still renting my appliances and washer and dryer and living from paycheck to paycheck. I had nothing but a bedroom set, and I had purchased two barstools for my new breakfast bar. My oldest daughter was married, and my youngest was living on her own. I had nothing and had been living that way for some time. I even rented the car I drove.

I struggled to pay the villa note and had no money set aside for a down payment to purchase it. I spent the rest of the time ducking the rental company men at the door, because I was behind on my weekly payments. As the year in the villa was drawing near I had to admit to myself again, and to the builder, that I would be unable to purchase the home and would have to find another place to live once again.

This was the 15th place I had lived in as an adult, and the instability of my existence was evident no matter how I wanted others to perceive something else about me. I moved into a two-bedroom apartment (because the villa got sold) and decided to give up on my dream of ever owning a home or feeling normal like everyone around me.

During this process, I started to turn my way back to God because I wasn't fulfilled, and He was faithful to speak a word of life to my spirit that stirred a fight within me not to give up.

January 5, 2010 - Prayer-Listening:

Look around this day and note where your life is because there is coming a time when you shall know it no more. Your latter shall be greater than your former. It will be a distant, vague memory. For the place, you see yourself, what I see and where I am taking you is so much better. For the thoughts, I have for you are greater than the thoughts you have toward yourself.

General Motors is soon to be done in your life because what I have is greater. Write these things down because as the days unfold before you, I will confirm my voice to you this day.

For the places that I am taking you are so great and different, you will look upon this day and not believe you were ever in this place.

I was given some furniture for my apartment, and I began to get serious about my walk with God. I started to seek a peace of mind and a solution to the madness, which summed up my life. I began to have some breakthroughs with saying NO to compromise with some men, but others (familiar spirits) could still push my buttons due to established soul ties not yet broken. I started shutting down the online dating websites as well. They were a buffet for the very indulgences that I was now tired of.

The man that I had previously been in an adulterous relationship with (*see chapter 2*), and had finally walked away from in 2006, came back into my life because he was losing his wife to a terminal illness. He wanted me to enter again into a compromising situation with him while he walked out this process with her and I said 'NO.' It was one of the most powerful times that I ever said 'NO.'

I loved this man and the way he treated me, but I no longer wanted a long-term connection as I started to consider God and His Word again. I would no longer be a surrogate lover for him and I told him to go home and take care of her.

At 51, I was still dysfunctional in so many areas of my life. I had been a born-again believer for 16 years by then, and the desire was to get free. I had to fight with every fiber of my being to know freedom in my mind, soul, and body, and to accept that God also wanted the same thing for me.

Slowly, the process of counseling with Dr. Kimberly gave me a safe place to start releasing my history without judgment. I saw the dots of some things connecting my life course so openly with her guidance, and I understood the things more clearly that were generationally sown. The greatest things I achieved were the learning tools I began to put in place as we trudged through the trenches of my war-torn soul to get my life on track for success.

> **Jeremiah 29:11,** For I know the thoughts and plans that I have for you, says the Lord, thoughts and plans for welfare and peace and not for evil, to give you hope in your outcome (AMP).

God had already told me that my latter would be greater than my former. We were making slow and deliberate progress. Unless one has had to fight in this realm of warfare (molestation & rape), they would not understand the madness you experience when your soul has been exposed through sexual violations and sins. God made clear in His Word what fornication, sexual sins and adultery can do to those who choose to practice these things. Then there are the layers of shame that envelops a wayward soul. This was my prayer continuously, "God you promised to restore my soul in Psalm 23:3."

> **Psalm 23: 3**, He refreshes and restores my life (myself); He leads me in the paths of righteousness [uprightness and right standing with Him—not for my earning it, but] for His name's sake (AMP).

I began to fight for celibacy during this time. I had to allow God to show me where boundaries needed to be restored in my life and home. Then came 2009, and I met a new type of man: I met a man of God and we hit it off instantly. Our connection was so different. I had made it almost a year since any sexual compromise, and I was strengthened in my relationship with God. My counseling was still going well, and I was doing well in submitting and supporting my pastors.

This man and I enjoyed spending time together and getting to know each other, and I thought he was going to be my husband. I had not asked God. Instead, I relied on our experiential time together and assumed because we both were Christians it was right. Since that time, I have learned that *two Christian people meeting is not a recipe for marriage without seeking God* through prayer and fasting to see if this is his plan for the both of you. Our desires rise, and we ignore everything to make it happen, sometimes to our detriment.

My advice is to run to the altar of God when you first meet a potential mate. Seek God and wait for Him to speak, He will let you know and save you a lot of time and possible devastation later.

We went back to our homes and lives with the understanding that we would be in touch and plan to get to know each other better. He was the first man I let my guard down for in a while, and because of his leadership position in the church, I placed my trust in that instead of God.

A few weeks later, I sensed this man was already dating someone else. He never volunteered the information, I had to ask. When I asked, he admitted he was seeing someone else, and I changed my number and cut him off instantly. I wanted to do right for once in my life. Though disappointed, I didn't fall apart this time; I was making progress little by little. I processed through it and went on with my life and continued growing in my relationship with God.

Eight months later, this man reached out to me through a mutual friend and I opened myself to dialogue with him. I was hopeful still that maybe there would be a chance if he were still single. After speaking for a while, I noticed he never brought up the relationship that he had with someone that caused me to walk away in the first place. I finally brought it up, and he admitted that he was engaged to be married to her. I was stunned and wanted to know why he had bothered to contact me. He said he missed our connection and wanted to maintain a friendship. I shared this with my pastors, and they warned me that this man's intentions were not right and to stay on guard.

I allowed the door of communication to remain an open door, which lead to more devastation. To medicate this new pain, I saw an opportunity to purchase a home on land contract. Here I go again for the third time, with a company that worked with people with less than perfect credit. I had a friend in another state that I was getting to know, so I threw him into the equation.

I heard the Holy Spirit tell me to 'be careful' when I was running around trying to make this house deal happen, and I was determined this time to feel better (my fix for normalcy) in light of this situation. I just knew if I got this house I would be okay. So, I put up the required $6000 down payment with the knowledge and understanding that if I didn't purchase the home within the year, I would lose the $6,000 period. I forged ahead with my heart of pain.

I loved the house because there was such peace in the home, the most peaceful place I had ever lived. I spent $4,000 more getting the basement set for whatever man I would marry and live in that house with. I bought the top of the line leather furniture, entertainment center, and created a bonafide man cave. I furnished the whole place and invited my daughter and my two granddaughters to live with me while we waited for the arrival of my second grandson. I was afraid to live in this big house with three floors by myself, so I created this family dynamic out of my need to feel normal.

I was still dysfunctional, broken and spiritually anemic throughout this process, but I didn't give up. Only two men ever stepped across the threshold of this home: the first was the former married man who ended up losing his wife to death. He came to see the house, and I wanted him to be proud of me. He was eight years older, and many times he was more of a father-type figure to me.

I knew deep down inside, I could never marry him now that he was a widower because of my guilt over the years of the affair. We discussed the possibility of joining together, but I just couldn't get past what we had already done. He came down for the day and spent time with me. The visit was peaceful because I was in a different place. For years, the only men I dealt with lived in other states, for some reason I was more comfortable that way.

The other visit came from my other friend who would come to visit his family, and there never was a compromise in our three and a half years of visiting back and forth. What I didn't realize, till a few years later after we parted ways, was that he was instrumental in helping me to establish a new dialogue with men. A NO compromise conversation.

Today, I have connections with some established men of God who are whole and without agendas. I found out there were men who were called to restore, protect, and re-establish respect toward women of God, as brothers and spiritual fathers. I love the men that God have sent across my path to help restore honor to me and show how a woman should be treated.

I never even noticed my progress until the year was up to buy the house, and once again I couldn't. First, the house was overpriced, and it would need significant remodeling. I was to blind to see these things until I moved in; I was too close to retirement years and thought how could I pay for new windows, a furnace, new driveway, plumbing work in the basement, and other things especially without a husband and being over 50 years old. I was starting to become more conscious of the years ahead of me and the stairs for laundry from the third level to the basement wore me out.

My failure faced me again for this third house I would not be able to own. I just did not do my homework ahead of time, especially since I had entered into all three homes in this chapter due to emotional pain. I was growing, though because I could go back to God and admit that I began this house deal with the wrong intents from my heart. I was nursing another broken heart and disappointment, and I trusted this process over trusting God to help heal my hurt. I owned my mistake and repented before God, and for once invited Him to lead my next move.

1 John 1:9, If we [freely] admit that we have sinned and confess our sins, He is faithful and just (true to His nature and promises) and will forgive our sins [dismiss our lawlessness] and [continuously] cleanse us from all unrighteousness [everything not in conformity to His will in purpose, thought, and action] (AMP).

It was in January 2011 that I needed a place to move again because I had to surrender the house. The rental company came and got the refrigerator, and the washer and dryer set; yes I was still renting some things including my car. Still working at General Motors, I had already sold the stove, and the 65" television. I only had a little money in the bank, but for the first time I had some, and I was worried about where my daughter and three grandbabies would go because I felt responsible for them as well. I had brought them into this life mess of mines.

The weight of the world was upon me. I sat in my car in the driveway in the dead of winter looking at this dream again slipping away, because I allowed my emotions to get me here over some man. I was trying to pull it together, because in a few hours I was heading to midnight prayer at the church. In that car, the tears and crying before the throne that evening could have rocked the universe, it was so violent and loud from within me. I had hit rock bottom. I was finally at the end of Iva.

While I was weeping, the Holy Spirit ever so gently said, "But this is the first home that you have lived in, and you never brought a man into your bed." I can clearly remember that moment in time. Then I screamed to my God as the reality of what God wanted me to see, past the money I would lose, and all the trappings attached to this house, I finally got a breakthrough which was more of the desire of my heart after years of praying and struggling to be free.

I cried, I screamed, and was in total disbelief that I was walking out a victory in this area finally. It had been 38 years since Joe sexually exploited me at 14 years of age and his signature on my soul (soul tie) was now being broken from the root.

I lived over half my life thinking that having a man was the epitome of living. If I didn't have one, I didn't like the emptiness that it created within me. I used my body as I had been taught to garner moments of superficial closeness if I couldn't experience the stability of a permanent relationship. I celebrated those that have had the gift and grace to marry and be with one person their entire life. I never blamed God for the brokenness of my marriages because His plan was a good one and that I believed.

Even today, I still embrace the beauty of marriages with longevity and a strong commitment to honor God and love one another. I have learned that following God's plan for your life will always produce fruits of peace and joy that are greater than the plan you had for yourself. My breakthrough finally manifested, and it has been almost eight years of reigning in this place of victory.

Today, I reside in the beautiful place the lord has blessed me with, surrounded by water and flowing fountains in the summer. The week I was moving into my new place, which was seven years ago, a set of events placed me before a man who sold cars. I purchased a vehicle, finally turned in the rental car, and noted the blessing of the $25 difference in my payments. Last year, I was able to purchase another car. The Lord promised a land flowing with milk and honey.

Here's the critical thing to know: before I moved into my current residence, the former married man I was involved with offered to provide a nice lump sum of money for me to move and get whatever I needed, no strings attached. Of course, at first, I said, "yes." But after thinking about it, I thought I wanted to trust God all the way even though I didn't know how I was going to afford another move so quickly.

I went back to him and said, "I decline your offer but thank you," and I turned my heart, hope, faith and every part of my being in prayer to God and said, "I am going to trust you, God, to meet every need to make this move possible. You brought me to this place of victory and the land flowing with milk and honey, Lord I need you to be able to cross over without any man's help, for the first time in my life this place will be dedicated to you and you alone."

The Message Bible describes the land flowing with milk and honey this way in **Exodus 3:7,8a, b**. God said:

"I've taken a good, long look at the affliction of my people in Egypt. I've heard their cries for deliverance from their slave masters; I know all about their pain. And now I have come down to help them, pry them loose from the grip of Egypt, get them out of that country and bring them to a good land with wide-open spaces, a land lush with milk and honey...".

This place has been without compromise. I kept my promise to God that this would be my place with Him alone as the head. I love the peace of no longer chasing behind the appetites of my flesh and being man obsessed. Even though a single man of God may pique my interest, I know to take that interest on any level back to God in prayer, and I am committed to God's response and guidance for me. The blessings have overtaken me, and God has made sure that I understood because I placed my trust in Him, He answered my prayer of faith.

This place I live in at the time of this writing is not a house, but it is a Christian home. I learned that I am woman enough to create a stable and anointed home. When I moved here, I was in a better place all around; no renting of anything, I was learning about finances and management on a level I never thought possible, and I am still growing in this area. I have been able to retire five years before my projected goal of 2021 just as God had promised (see journal entry above) due to some significant financial blessings that included the return of the $10,000 I had lost from the last house.

God has provided everything in my life to make it possible to live normal, and He did it without me dwelling in a house or having a husband. Boundaries have been restored and new ones have been established, and my self-respect is back in place.

I look around sometimes and marvel at this place of contentment in my life after where I have been. I have everything I need, and that is a fantastic feeling.

> **Philippian 4:11 – 13, (AMP)**
> Not that I speak from [any personal] need, for I have learned to be content [and self-sufficient through Christ, satisfied to the point where I am not disturbed or uneasy] regardless of my circumstances.
>
> 12. I know how to get along and live humbly [in difficult times], and I also know how to enjoy abundance and live in prosperity. In any and every circumstance I have learned the secret [of facing life], whether well-fed or going hungry, whether having an abundance or being in need.
>
> 13. I can do all things [which He has called me to do] through Him who strengthens and empowers me [to fulfill His purpose-----I am self-sufficient in Christ's sufficiency; I am ready for anything and equal to anything through Him who infuses me with inner strength and confident peace.]

Once again, my purpose for sharing my story was to help others struggling with deep roots of shame and inner pain, so that God can restore what was lost. Your age means absolutely nothing; I am preparing to celebrate my 60th birthday in a couple months as the Lord's wills. My latter has been so much greater than from where I started. These past few years of my life have been ***His restoration power in motion***.

Chapter Six

THE PROMISE
God's Redemption Plan for You

The day I became a born-again believer of the Gospel of Jesus Christ, and received Him into my life as my personal Lord and Savior, was my best decision ever.

I was 35 years old and didn't understand, at first, how powerful this decision would be for my family and me. My life was being transformed. I encountered a very real, supernatural God of truth who redeemed my life from the path to hell I was on.

Our Heavenly Father loved us so much that He gave His son to the world, so that who ever believes in Him would not die but would have everlasting life. *For God did not send His Son into the world to condemn the world, but to save the world through him (John 3:16-17 NIV).*

No matter what has happened in your life up until this hour, God gave you His Son, so you can receive Him and allow Him to transform your life. You may wonder how this works? How do you obtain this amazing gift into your life?

First, you must understand why you need to have Christ as the head of your life. Let me speak for me, I couldn't figure things out for myself, and I tried for the longest time. My life was a complete mess, while I longed for something greater and the juggling act had gotten quite old. Then, I found out the gift of the Son was to give me more of an abundant life.

> **John 10:10** (AMP) The thief comes only to steal and kill and destroy. I came that they may have and enjoy life, and have it in abundance (to the full, till it overflows).

With the abundant life comes freedom from shame and guilt. God gave His Son Jesus who died for the sins we have committed. He shed His blood as payment to the Father for our sins. Once we are in Christ Jesus, there is no condemnation (*read Romans 8:1; Isaiah 54:4*). The former mindsets and beliefs are no more when we are walking in the spirit. I know this to be true.

You just read my story, and I no longer live under the shame and condemnation of my former life. I walk in the confidence of the amazing gift of Jesus Christ. He is more than enough. I could do nothing to earn or work for this gift of salvation. It is free. The only requirement is that I believe that Jesus Christ is the only acceptable Savior to a dying world.

At first, I had to fight to believe this, but my faith became stronger as I walked this journey and I never want to live any other way. My entire past has been forgiven along with the shame and guilt. *"A Yucky Dialog"* is my story of life more abundantly.

When you receive Jesus as your Lord and Savior, the Bible shares the entire benefit package with us when we join the Kingdom of God. God loves you. He knows everything that you have done and what has brought you the greatest shame. He already knew, and yet He still loved you and is offering you something greater. Are you ready to unwrap this amazing gift of love that God has for you, which is Jesus Christ? (***John 10:9-13***)

Let us pray this prayer right now while your reading this:

Heavenly Father,

*I thank you for this moment in time. I recognize that I need you now more than ever. I confess my sins before You and ask You to forgive me. I have lived according to my way, but today I want to start living the best life you have for me. "I confess to you with my mouth (that Jesus is Lord) and I believe in my heart That You raised Him from the dead and because I believe, I am saved" (**John 10:9**). Thank you for this gift of your Son. Now Lord lead me to a church where your Word is taught, and where your Holy Spirit dwells that I may grow in this walk with you. Send true believers across my path daily to help mature me in the things of God. Thank you for my new abundant life.*

In Jesus Christ Name, Amen

Chapter Seven

Healing Expressions

Healing Expressions is a group of poetic writings that I have done throughout the years to express my heart in moments of deep reflection.

Each one also is in correlation to some incident in the book. Included first is the submission from my youngest daughter Giavanna Smith who was also sexually violated. I am so honored to share her heart with you as she continues in her journey of healing and wholeness.

We hope you enjoy our expressions!

RECLAIMING ME

Don't judge me,
you don't know how early my sexuality was stolen from me by men who never should have noticed me
You don't know how long being a female disgusted me because I thought boys had it easy (oh how misguided that was)
I was raised to close my legs, and not wear anything too tight cause men were around
But these lessons didn't help me, men flocked to me like a wolf to its prey
Took what I didn't even know I had

You don't know how many nights I prayed for God to just end it all because I didn't want to be a victim anymore
You don't know what that last rape broke in me
You don't know how betrayed by my body I felt
If you've never been lost in your skin you can't decide how I reclaim mine
You can't judge me falling in love with every wrinkle and crease that covers me
You don't have a right to project your insecurities on me just because I chose to celebrate my sexuality freely
You've never had to reclaim yours

Written August 1, 2018 by Giavanna (Gigi) Smith, All rights reserved

PONDERING:

IF I WERE TO PONDER:
This life that seems so hurried to pass me by,
Daily choices and decisions that I recall,
My broken heart and confusion from this terminal mind.

IF I WERE TO PONDER:
Every mistake and failure that marks my unsettled soul,
With only a tiny glimmer of hope that emerges from a distant horizon.

IF I WERE TO PONDER:
The tomorrow that is not promised,
The yesterday that was craftily stolen from me,
Or the today that tick tocks.... tick tocks......tick tocks.......
What can I change?

IF I WERE TO PONDER:
The lost irretrievable innocence of my youth,
The gradual aim of a sadistic marksman, and the assignment to destroy
my life in the lowest of ways.

IF I WERE TO PONDER:
The tender seductive eyes of loves first encounter,
Before the lies of forever and forever,
And the knocks of betrayals that often follows.

NOW WHEN I PONDER:

A new birth that daily lights my way,
A love of Christ that challenges the lies of my past,
The new identity that establishes and shouts out,
Who I am.........Who's I am.

NOW WHEN I PONDER:
The new prospect of my life,
The genuine smiles of love that envelopes me on my daily journeys,
The dreams and hopes of my present...............and YES, my future.

NOW WHEN I PONDER:
God's constant renewal of His continued unconditional mercies, grace and love,
My cup is full........ I rejoice....... YES, I rejoice.
Thank you, Lord, that despite myself,
I reign in the strength of your light.

Just Stretch............Just Walk.......... Just Breathe............
Just. Sing.............. Just. Laugh.........Just Praise HIM.......................
Just Worship HIM!

For HE is eternally worthy...WHEN I PONDER!

Written May 4, 2006 by Iva J. Brassfield, All rights reserved

WHAT IS YOUR NAME?
John 4: 4 - 28

Woman at Jacob's Well....... What is your name?
Who me? ...
Yes, you, so consumed with your pain.
My name?
It's been lost over time under layers of shame.
I've been busy searching you see,
Looking for love and fulfillment in many arms, that would be me.

My name? I don't know.......why can't you just let me be?
My name....... it's been lost over time
Somewhere between husband #1, #2 or was it husband #3

For I have a story to tell, as so many do,
If you'll just sit for one moment, I'll explain it to you.
My heart had a hole, the size I do not know,
No one could fill it
No one could fix it,
I searched to and FRO.
Then one day in my thirst, I found a real man,
Different from all the others,
Surely it must be a DIVINE plan.

He spoke of my thirst that no man had been able to quench,

Then he offered me the living water of life that finally calmed my soul's stench.
Who is this one who could know so much about me?
I now know the one at Jacob's Well,
He was waiting all along for me.
Waiting there patiently to set my heart, my soul, my emotions, and my body free.

My new name is Redeemed……. bought with a price can't you see?
I've been washed in the Blood of Jesus,
I've been totally set free.

No more hungering,
No more thirsting,
No more sleeping in all the wrong places.
Soliciting false hope and love,
Peering up into unknown faces.
The light of my life has been revealed unto me,
He is now known
His name is JESUS and he is the one who Redeemed me……
He fulfilled me,
He cleansed me
And now I have been made whole.
The beginning of my true story, is ready to unfold.

Woman at Jacob's Well……What is your name?
Who me?

Yes you......now where was that pain?

My name.........is now REDEEMED

FREE FROM LAYERS OF SHAME

Yes, REDEEMED and that's what I now can proclaim!

Written February 28, 2003 by Iva J Brassfield

OLD PAIN

Wells of tears pour forth out of me, deeper than the bowels of
the earth.

Years of turn away go away another day

Bleed out of a heart that has been rejected time and time again.

Pour out old pain, old shame, old misery,

Pour out for this is no longer your place of habitation.

Your place old pain is not to flow freely through my veins
clogging up my life,

Drowning out my life,

Encamping in the depths of my bowels to keep the toxic waste
of your poisons in.

Give up your place old pain,

For you're not welcomed or wanted here any longer,

Your deception, your death..........

LIFE flow in my inner most being,

HOPE rise as a sparkling sword within me, to cut loose all roots of pain.

PEACE, be the river of life that touches every heartbeat that flows throughout my body, my mind, my soul.

Written 1998 by Iva J. Brassfield, all rights reserved

Can you SEE me?

All my life been chasing behind some man.
Like a love starved somebody saying to each man......
Are you the one who will love me, are you he?
Please somebody come love me,
Just stop using me.
If you will love me I will do whatever you want,
say what you need with my lips that flatter.
just please come love me before I die.

Will some man please just love me?
I am worth love.
Just don't ask me about my secrets,
Don't want folks to know, been hiding for a long while,
Been keeping your secrets in me to.
Round the way kinda girl you say,
then why you always come to play?

Can you SEE me?

Please tell me that you can SEE me.

No one else does.

Dress up, dress down.

Can you SEE me man?

Can you SEE me?

Written June 18, 2011 by Iva J Brassfield,

LETTING GO

A thought of regret in the mind,

Is like the irritation of a slow deliberate drop of water from a leaky faucet. You seek the handle of release, to stop that constant reminder that something is amiss. So is a past that has reigned in the mind over the years of replay after replay.

Hurts, wounds, bad choices, failures, disappointments, lies, betrayals, falsehoods, broken dreams, unfilled desires……………. sounds like drip, drip, drip, drip. Time waits, hesitates or stops for NO man,

You stop living in that moment of "each" incident;

Encased like a mouse held back in a trap…………. scratch, scratch, scratch. There is no going forward and there is no turning back…. drip, drip, drip, and drip.

Year (drip), after year (drip), after agonizing year (drip) is the minds dance of remembrance.

Now old age has ascended and clothed you like the perfect fit of
a new garment,
And you lay there trying to recapture time long gone.
Through the hush of that moment you can still hear
it...........drip.... drip.... drip.

You encourage the body to rise and give it one more try,
As you move slowly to the minds leaky faucet,
the solution becomes so clear as you rush to stop the dripping of
thoughts one after another.
By any means you regain your solitude, your peace,
You restore your inner sanctity, you release and let go of the
past......

LETTING GO-------------------starts in the mind. And it's never too
late to RELEASE & LET GO!

Written May 7, 2006 by Iva J. Brassfield, all rights reserved

MY DANCE, MY KING

(For every woman with the dream of being Cinderella in her heart.)

Can I have this dance MY KING?
That moment in your gentle arms of love, to escape the reality
of my being,
Just one quiet dance with MY KING,
One moment to exhale the frailty of my existence,

One moment to dance away all shame.

Can I have this dance MY KING?
You who will protect me in your arms of power,
Who sees me for who I truly am,
Gliding me across the dance floor into my destiny with YOU,
uninhabited by my past.

MY KING is the KING OF KINGS,
MY KING is the LORD of LORDS,
And HE reigns in SPLENDOR and MAJESTY.

No place I would rather be then taking my dance with MY KING.
MY KING....JESUS CHRIST who reigns FOREVER!

Written December 2, 2016 by Iva J Brassfield, all rights reserved

RESOURCE PAGE

A. National Sexual Assault Hotline
    1-800-656-4673 [24/7 hotline]

B. National Child Abuse Hotline
    1-800-422-4453

C. National Human Trafficking Hotline
    1-888-373-7888

D. National Suicide Prevention Lifeline
    1-800-273-Talk (8255) [24/7 hotline)
    1-888-628-9454 (Spanish)
    1-800-799-4889 (TTY)

E. National Hotline for Crime Victims
    1-855-4-Victim (1-855-484-2846)

F. 1in6 Online Support Groups
    (Support Groups for Male Survivors of Childhood Sexual
    Abuse and Adult Sexual Assault [free, anonymous].)
    1in6 Online Helpline/www.1in6.org

G. Human Trafficking and Social Justice Institute
    University of Toledo
    Toledo. Ohio
    (419) 530-5590
    www.utoledo.edu

About the Author

Iva J Brassfield, (*Simply IvaB*) is a licensed and ordained Elder under New Directions Church International in Southfield, Michigan. She previously served as UAW Local 14 Chaplain while working at the Powertrain General Motors plant in Toledo, Ohio until her retirement in 2016.

Earning her Master's in Theology from the North Carolina Theological Seminary in 2018, Iva's mandate is to help people overcome the challenges of this life through a consistent and reliable relationship with Jesus Christ. She desires to see everyone experience genuine resurrection power in their everyday living; no background is too degrading (yucky) for restoration.

She is the mother of two daughters, one dynamic son-in-love, and five grandchildren whom she calls her 'Five Heartbeats.' She resides in Ohio.

The meaning of Y.U.C.K.Y. comes from the following:

Yielding

Under

Christ the

King

Yokes of Bondage

CONTACT INFORMATION FOR THE AUTHOR

Email: theyuckyd@gmail.com
Phone: (855) 372-0500
Instagram: Simply_IvaB
Website: www.theyuckyd.com

Iva Brassfield
P.O. Box 874
Sylvania, Ohio 43560-9998

Made in the USA
Middletown, DE
26 January 2022

58631392R00086